A Century of Change

THE YOUNG OXFORD HISTORY OF
BRITAIN & IRELAND

A Century of Change

1900~2000

JAMES MASON

General Editor
PROFESSOR KENNETH O. MORGAN

OXFORD
UNIVERSITY PRESS

OXFORD
UNIVERSITY PRESS

Great Clarendon Street, Oxford OX2 6DP

Oxford University Press is a department of the University of Oxford.
It furthers the University's objective of excellence in research, scholarship,
and education by publishing worldwide in

Oxford New York

Athens Auckland Bangkok Bogotá Buenos Aires
Cape Town Chennai Dar es Salaam Delhi Florence Hong Kong Istanbul
Karachi Kolkata Kuala Lumpur Madrid Melbourne Mexico City Mumbai
Nairobi Paris São Paulo Shanghai Singapore Taipei Tokyo Toronto Warsaw

with associated companies in Berlin Ibadan

Oxford is a registered trade mark of Oxford University Press
in the UK and in certain other countries

Text copyright © James Mason 2001
Illustrations copyright © Oxford University Press 2001

The moral rights of the author/artist have been asserted
Database right Oxford University Press (maker)

First published 2001
Some material in this book was previously published in
The Young Oxford History of Britain & Ireland 1996

British Library Cataloguing in Publication Data available

Paperback ISBN 0–19–910832-3

1 3 5 7 9 10 8 6 4 2

Designed by Richard Morris, Stonesfield Design
Printed in Malaysia

CONTENTS

❖

CHAPTER 1

Land of hope and glory

❖

(above) A postcard advertising soap. Postcards first appeared in 1899. They were issued by the big firms which relied on the empire for their imported tea, cocoa, soap and cigarettes.

(left) A map of the British Empire (the areas in pink) in the reign of Edward VII. It was the largest empire in history, covering one fifth of the world's land surface.

The people of Britain celebrated New Year's Day and the start of the twentieth century on Tuesday 1 January 1901. Three weeks later they were mourning the death of Queen Victoria. She had been on the throne for 37 years. A children's book written in that year described how 'the nation received a shock deeper seated than any other which the country had known ... The nation mourned as one great family for its head.'

The new monarch, her son Edward VII (1901–1910) was crowned not only 'King of the United Kingdom of Great Britain and Ireland' but also King 'of the British dominions beyond the seas, ... Emperor of India'. The British Empire was the largest in the world and the British entered the century apparently proud and confident. It was Edward VII who suggested that words should be set to the first 'Pomp and Circumstance' march recently composed by Edward Elgar. The result, performed in 1902, was 'Land of Hope and Glory'. Almost at once it became a second national anthem:

Land of Hope and Glory, Mother of the Free
How shall we extol thee, who are born of thee?
Wider still and wider shall thy bounds be set;
God who made thee mighty, make thee mightier yet.

Britain and the world

The poet and novelist, Rudyard Kipling, caught the spirit of this huge trading empire in a poem which he wrote for a school history book:

Oh, where are you going to, all you Big Steamers,
With England's own coal, up and down the salt seas?
We are going to fetch you your bread and your butter,
Your beef, pork and mutton, eggs, apples, and cheese.

In fact the steamers were as likely to be burning Welsh or Scottish coal as English. The South Wales coalfield alone produced nearly a fifth of all British coal. The ships which docked in Cardiff and Glasgow, London and Liverpool were built in the shipyards of Belfast and Aberdeen, on the banks of the Clyde, on Merseyside, Tyneside and in Barrow. The trade with the empire reached into every region of the United Kingdom.

Not everyone, however, thought Britain's position in the world was as secure as it had once been. Her rivals for empire were enlarging their armies and Germany was starting to build a navy. 'If the German Fleet becomes superior to ours,' said the First Lord of the Admiralty in 1902, 'the German army can conquer this country'. The race to gain naval superiority had begun.

The British were also aware that their leading industrial position was under threat, particularly from the United States of America and Germany. Britain had been the first country to have an 'industrial revolution'. As other countries industrialized too, her lead was bound to be challenged. Would British manufacturers manage to keep up with the competition, and would they be as good as their rivals at making the latest products such as electrical goods and motor cars?

A 1911 Royal Navy 'Dreadnought' Battleship. The British Royal Navy responded to the German naval threat by commissioning a new type of battleship. Dreadnoughts were an example of all that was new in technological developments. The fastest battleships afloat, they were driven by turbine engines and their ten long-range guns could sink an enemy vessel while staying clear of a torpedo attack. They also used wireless communication, recently pioneered by Guglielmo Marconi. The Germans responded by building their own version.

In some industries Britain held her own. In 1913 she was still the leading shipbuilder, making half of all new steam ships in the world and, although the USA remained the leading manufacturer of motor vehicles, Britain's factories turned out more cars, trucks and buses than Germany's.

Days of gaiety

For the rich, life at the beginning of the twentieth century was more comfortable and enjoyable than it had ever been. Their large houses in cities and towns provided work for many servants; in 1901 there were over two million servants in Britain. The Marchioness Curzon of Kedleston, who belonged to the very richest landowning group, referred to as 'Society', described how she,

> always had a large house party for Ascot Races, and all our friends had people staying with them too, and there were dinner parties and balls every night during race week. These full days of gaiety involved rapid changes of dress. We wore chiffon and lace dresses at Ascot with large picture hats.

They ate good food and rode, danced and hunted. Motoring was a rich man's hobby and the sight of a car could bring out a whole village to stare. It brought to an end the silence of the countryside. One man, Mont Abbott, who lived in the village of Enstone in Oxfordshire, remembered how,

In that heyday of the railways, before many motors come about, the main roads through villages were often deserted for hours on end.... Squire Faulkner was supposed to have had the first motor in Enstone... It terrified horses so whenever a horse approached he had to stop, and his gardener ran behind to push and help him to start it again.

(above) A poster for the first production of J.M. Barrie's play, Peter Pan, *which opened in London in December 1904. The story was published as a book in 1911. Other books for children published around this time became very popular.*

Among them were Rudyard Kipling's Kim *(1901), and his* Just So Stories *(1902), all set in India (*The Jungle Book *had already appeared in 1894); Beatrix Potter's* Tale of Peter Rabbit *was published in 1902 and Kenneth Grahame's* Wind in the Willows *in 1908.*

(below) At the races, 1909. Members of the aristocracy, and other rich families, enjoyed the events of the

social season, which included horse-racing at Ascot, rowing at Henley and sailing at Cowes.

The Motor Car

▼ As adverts like this one showed, in the 1930s car owners could go away for weekend trips and holidays almost wherever they wished. Summer holiday traffic jams, and petrol stations beside the roads, became a common sight.

'I am told', said Queen Victoria, speaking of cars in the 1890s, 'that they smell exceedingly nasty, and are very shaky and disagreeable conveyances altogether.' Yet within a hundred years motor vehicles had transformed the everyday lives of the British people, and the landscape in which they lived and worked.

Until the 1920s cars were a luxury few could afford. Then the introduction of assembly lines by car manufacturers made cars cheaper to make and, therefore, also cheaper to buy. Many middle-class families bought their first car between the wars. They still mostly travelled to work by bus and train, using the car for leisure trips.

In the 1950s and 1960s even more people could afford a car, and thousands were employed in the factories where they were made. Now people began to rely on cars for work, leisure and shopping. Families with a car could also move out of the city centres, into the new suburbs or even the country, where public transport services were declining.

▶ In the 1920s William Morris brought the assembly line method of car production to Britain, from the USA. Specialist firms made the different components of the cars, which were then assembled at Morris's factory at Cowley, in Oxford.

Companies began to use lorries, rather than trains, to transport their goods. In 1959 Britain's first motorway, the M1, was opened to carry fast, long-distance traffic. In the 1960s, as cars and buses drew people away from the railways, about a quarter of the railway network was closed. The people without cars were isolated.

By the 1990s many people were concerned about the cost to the environment, and to society, of so many people having private cars. Although cars brought people individual freedom, new road schemes were destroying the countryside, the towns were clogged up with traffic, and fumes from vehicle exhausts were damaging people's health. In large cities like Sheffield and Manchester, modern tram systems were introduced as fast, cheap and clean alternatives to the car.

▲ By 1990 there were just over 3000 kilometres of motorway in use in Britain. Motorways have made a huge impact on both the look of the landscape and its plants and wildlife. Work went ahead here, at Twyford Down in Hampshire, even though the area was home to rare plants and butterflies, and set aside as a Site of Special Scientific Interest.

▲ By the end of the century people were driving to large supermarkets like this one on the outskirts of towns, to do their shopping. The shops in the town centres suffered, and so did the environment.

▼ The Morris Minor was a classic British car. It was first produced in 1948 as a two-door saloon. By 1961, one million Morris Minors had been made.

The invention of the aero-plane revolutionized both transport and communications in the new century. In 1903 the American brothers Orville and Wilbur Wright made the first powered flight. In 1909 a Frenchman, Louis Blériot, made the first flight across the English Channel. This photograph shows him just after he landed, at Dover Castle. His flight from Sangatte, near Calais, took forty-three minutes.

Technology and change

By 1914 there were 140,000 cars on British roads and other inventions of the 1890s were also beginning to change the way many people lived their day-to-day lives. Those who could afford them bought telephones and typewriters for their offices. Faraday's discovery of electricity was put to work to provide light and power. In Liverpool an overhead electric railway was built to run the length of the docks and in 1903 London had its first electric tram.

(below) An advertisement for a gas cooker. Although electricity replaced it for lighting homes, gas remained important for cooking and heating.

The new trams linked city centres to the fast-growing suburbs where middle-class families moved to buy new comfortable homes with electric lighting instead of gas, more rooms and large gardens. The writer J.B.Priestley described

(right) An office scene in the early 1900s. Although British businesses were slow to take up the invention of the type-writer, the use of typewriters and telephones in offices created more opportunities for educated girls. They began to take over secretarial and administrative jobs from male clerks.

how the house which his family bought for £550 when they left the city for the suburbs had,

> a kitchen where we ate when we were by ourselves, a front room, where we ate when we had company, a smaller and gloomier back room, a bathroom on the half landing, two bedrooms and two attics.

The Central London Railway opened in 1905. It was one of several new all-electric lines to be built in tubes deep under London.

The new trams also improved life for working class families with secure jobs. One Londoner writing in about 1906 described the new freedom given by,

> fast lines of electric trams, brilliantly lighted, in which reading is a pleasure ... Each workman today in [Camberwell] has had an hour added to his life ... family after family are evacuating the blocks and crowded tenements for little four-roomed cottages with little gardens, at Hither Green or Tooting.

For most working class people life in cities began to have more variety. There was sport to go to on Saturday afternoon, cricket and football being especially popular. Music halls flourished, although challenged by the first silent films which drew away ever larger audiences. The first purpose-built cinema in the world opened in Colne in Lancashire in 1907.

The public house was often the centre of community life. Larger pubs were built and impressive plate glass mirrors and better lighting made them brighter places. Drink continued to ruin the lives of many but the amount of alcohol drunk began to fall from the huge amounts consumed in the late nineteenth century. Smoking, on the other hand, increased, especially among children.

Poverty and reform

For the many working class people without secure jobs, life remained a battle against grinding poverty. In 1901 people were shocked by evidence of how widespread this was when Seebohm Rowntree published the results of his enquiries into how people lived in York, where his Quaker family owned the chocolate factory. The report, *Poverty, A Study of Town Life,* explained how one in four families had to spend what money they had on bare necessities:

> They must never spend a penny on a railway fare or omnibus ... they must never purchase a half-penny newspaper or spend a penny to buy a ticket for a popular concert ... they must never ... give anything to a neighbour which costs them money. The children must not have pocket money or dolls or sweets or marbles ... finally the wage earner must never be absent from his work for a single day.

Among the many who read it was a young MP, Winston Churchill. 'I can see little glory in an empire which can rule the waves and is unable to flush the sewers', he wrote afterwards.

Ploughing in the early 1900s. Horses continued to provide most of the power on farms until the 1940s. Daily life in the countryside was often portrayed as happy and healthy, but wages were often low and life was hard for many families.

For those who worked in the countryside daily life changed little. Men worked on the land and many young girls went into 'service' as domestic servants. Poverty was as bad as it was in the towns. Mont Abbott remembered how his family struggled to pay the rent: 'paying Jinny the rent were a weekly do', and being hungry meant that,

> we walked afar on little food, our boots was always miles from our stomachs. We was glad to yut [eat] anything, going hunting at night with a lantern ... netting the 'poor man's game' the roosting blackies, thrushers and spajits.

In the early years of the century the Liberal government, elected in 1906, tried new ways of helping the very poor. In 1908 Lloyd George's Old Age Pensions Act provided a weekly pension for men and women over seventy which, for many, meant the difference between old age in the workhouse or a poor but independent life in their own small home. In 1909 new offices, called Labour Exchanges, started to provide information about job vacancies. In 1911 Lloyd George's National Insurance Act set up a scheme to provide all workers with pay and medical treatment if they were ill.

The 'people's budget'

The Liberals' reforms were popular but expensive. In his 1909 'people's budget' speech, the Chancellor of the Exchequer, Lloyd George, proposed new taxes on the very rich and on the profits of those who owned land. The Conservatives, many of whom were landowners, were horrified. They used their majority in the House of Lords to defeat the 'people's budget'.

Traditionally decisions about money were a matter for the Commons, so the Liberals immediately called a general election. They won and the

Lords backed down; but the government was now determined to pass the Parliament Bill, in order to reduce their power for good. When the new king, George V (1910–1936) backed the Prime Minister, Herbert Asquith, and promised that, if necessary, he would create enough Liberal peers to outvote the Conservatives in the Lords, they gave in and accepted the Bill.

The unions and the Labour Party

At the start of the twentieth century the trade unions faced a crisis which put at risk their very existence. They thought they had won the right to strike without being prosecuted (provided there was no violence) under Disraeli's government in 1875. Successful strikes by the match girls and the dockers had been followed by others and new unions, including ones for railwaymen and miners, had been formed. Then, in 1901, a single court case threatened to destroy their most important weapon. The Taff Vale Railway Company in Wales took the Amalgamated Society of Railway Servants to court, claiming that the union should pay for the company's losses caused by a strike. Although every union believed it had the right to strike by law, the court agreed with the company.

Only Parliament could establish this right once and for all. So the unions began to support the Labour Representation Committee (LRC), set up in 1900. In the election of 1906 the LRC and working-class candidates standing as Liberals together won fifty-four seats. The two groups of MPs combined and called themselves the Labour Party. They supported the Liberals' Trades Disputes Act which gave back to the unions the right to strike without being taken to court for the financial cost to an employer.

In the early 1900s there was plenty of work in factories and mines, but wages were low. Unions, which now had the right to strike in law and a booming membership, were in a strong position to demand better wages and improved working hours. Between 1910 and 1912 a series of strikes swept through nearly every major industry. Afraid there would be violence, the government used troops to support the police to control the strikers. Winston Churchill, the Home Secretary, was to be branded for the rest of his life in the mining valleys of South Wales as the man who sent the troops against the miners of Tonypandy in 1910. A year later troops shot and killed two workers at Llanelli during a national railway strike. To many it appeared that Britain was on the verge of a class war.

Police and troops escorting a convoy through a gathering of strikers in Liverpool, 1911.

A suffragette poster, 1909.

'Deeds not words'

As the Liberal government caught the mood of change in the country, another group demanded reform. Women still could not vote for an MP nor stand for Parliament and many were becoming ever more frustrated. In the 1880s Mrs Millicent Fawcett's National Union of Women's Suffrage Societies, believed they would win the right to vote by patient argument. Mrs Emmeline Pankhurst, with her daughters Christabel and Sylvia, disagreed. Angry that Parliament refused even to debate the issue of women's suffrage, they argued for militant action. In 1903 they started a breakaway group, the Women's Social and Political Union (WSPU), soon known as the 'suffragettes'. Their motto was 'Deeds not Words'.

They organized public meetings and marches, and interrupted political meetings to draw attention to their cause. In 1906 they hoped the new Liberal government would listen but the Prime Minister, Sir Henry Campbell-Bannerman, advised patience. 'We have been patient too long. We will be patient no longer', Mrs Pankhurst told a crowd of six thousand in Trafalgar Square.

Angry suffragettes turned to violent protest, throwing bricks through shop windows and burning letter boxes and buildings. Although some disapproved and left, the campaign drew attention to women's demands as never before. The number of Women's Suffrage Societies grew from seventy in 1909 to four hundred by 1913. In that year Emily Davison ran into the path of King George V's racehorse at the Epsom Derby, shouting 'Votes for Women'. Badly injured, she died a few days later. In London, ten bands and a guard-of-honour of over two thousand women escorted her coffin through streets lined with spectators.

Camden High Street, London, 1908. By 1901 women had won the right to take part in local government and to enter some universities and professions, such as medicine and accountancy. But they were still barred from the law and the Civil Service.

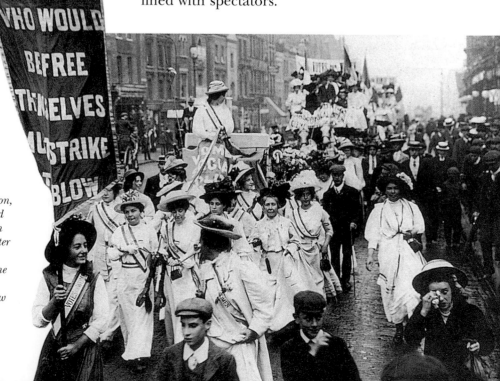

Home Rule at last?

Ireland entered the twentieth century with the question of Home Rule still unresolved. The arguments between its supporters and opponents were becoming ever more dangerous. At Westminster, the Liberals depended not only on the support of the new Labour Party but also on that of the Irish Party, now united under a new leader, John Redmond. His price for supporting the government was Home Rule for Ireland, which the Liberals favoured but the Conservatives, now known as the Conservative and Unionist Party, opposed.

Ulster Protestants were also bitterly opposed to Home Rule. The northern province produced ninety per cent of Ireland's manufactured goods, and Britain was its main market. Protestant workers, often using violence, had managed to drive Catholics out of the better paid jobs. Under Home Rule they would lose these advantages and become subject to a government based in Dublin and dominated by Catholics.

In 1912, when Asquith presented his Home Rule Bill to Parliament, nearly half a million Ulster people, led by Sir Edward Carson, signed a solemn covenant, or agreement, promising to use 'all means ... to defeat the present conspiracy to set up Home Rule for Ireland', even if that meant using armed force. In 1913 they set up an Ulster Volunteer force; the Irish nationalists created the Irish National volunteers. Ireland seemed on the brink of civil war.

Sir Edward Carson inspecting loyalist volunteers in Ulster in 1912. Carson was a clever, well-known Dublin lawyer. At a unionist rally in July in England he said that the government could 'tell us if they like that this is treason. It is not for men who have such stakes as we have at issue to trouble about the cost. We are prepared to take the consequences and in the struggle we shall not be alone, because we have all the best in England with us'.

The trumpet call of war

Throughout the early years of the century the rivalries between the countries of Europe for empire and trade had created international crisis after crisis, and the great powers had split into two camps, with Britain, France and Russia in one and Germany, Austria-Hungary (and later Turkey) in the other. It needed only a spark to ignite an explosion. It came when the Austrian archduke and his wife were shot dead by a Bosnian Serb in Sarajevo. Austria declared war on Serbia, and the allies of the two countries immediately came to their aid. Germany's invasion of Belgium, as part of a plan to attack France, then brought Britain into the war, since she had a longstanding agreement to defend Belgium against aggressors.

On Tuesday 4 August 1914, the Prime Minister announced that the United Kingdom and its empire were at war with Germany. 'The lamps

A recruiting poster for the British army. By October 1915 the government had managed to attract 2.25 million volunteers.

are going out all over Europe', said the Foreign Secretary, Sir Edward Grey. 'We shall not see them lit again in our lifetime.' Yet the public greeted the outbreak of war with excitement, 'thrilling', in the words of the poet, W.N. Hodgson, 'to the trumpet call of war'. Outside Parliament a journalist saw streets,

> thronged with people highly excited and rather boisterous ... All were already touched with war fever. They regarded their country as a crusader – redressing all wrongs and bringing freedom to the oppressed nations. Cries of 'Down with Germany' were raised.

Stirred by patriotism, and convinced that this was a just war, young men throughout the United Kingdom and the empire responded to the government's call for volunteers. Rich and poor joined up as one nation, burying their differences as they flocked to join the forces. In Oxfordshire Mont Abbott could remember every detail of the scene as the men of his village joined up outside the pub:

> Now they be mustering in earnest under the old elm on the green opposite the Litchfield: the best of labourers, the best of horses, the cream of the land. I can see them still as they were on

that summer's day in 1914, laughing and calling their farewells, under the starter's orders, then clattering off in a band up the village, charging for foreign parts and Charlbury Station.

CHAPTER 2

Your country needs you

❖

Daddy, what did **YOU** do in the Great War?

Until 1916, when it introduced compulsory military service, the government used posters like this to persuade men to join up. Some people, known as 'conscientious objectors', refused to fight because they believed it was wrong to kill, even in war.

In the face of war a spirit of unity spread across the land. Trade union leaders pledged their support for the war. In Ireland Redmond called upon the National Volunteers to enlist in the army while Carson offered a force of Ulster Volunteers. The WSPU ceased its activities and the Pankhursts proceeded to recruit men and women to help to win a war most people said would be 'over by Christmas'. The Scottish newspaper, *The Stirling Journal*, reflected the enthusiasm,

> The appeal for recruits to join the colours at this anxious time has been nobly responded to, and since the outbreak of hostilities men have been flocking to enlist at the depot, Argyll and Sutherland Highlanders, Stirling Castle.

Over a million had joined up by Christmas.

A new kind of war

Soldiers of the British Expeditionary Force (BEF), Britain's regular army, crossed the Channel to join up with the larger Belgian and French forces to stop the German advance. Four months later the BEF had all but ceased to exist. The Germans forced the Allies to retreat. Then they turned to hold the line. At the first Battle of Ypres the casualties were a sign of what was to come in a war that made use of all the new

technology available. About fifty thousand British soldiers were killed or wounded. French casualties were also heavy, and the Germans' even worse. By November 1914 both sides had dug themselves into deep trenches, along a front line running across Europe from the Belgian coast to Switzerland. As Christmas approached the war settled into deadlock.

At first the public thought the war would be short and glorious, but soon it became all too aware of the grim realities of modern warfare, as vast armies pounded one another daily with a barrage of heavy artillery fire on a scale never before experienced. Exploding shells created a landscape of churned mud, water-filled craters and shattered trees, killing and maiming terrified soldiers. Many men, one survivor recalled, went 'through severe torture and would cower down holding their heads in their hands, moaning and trembling'. Poets such as William Gibson recorded the routines of survival and sudden death,

We ate our breakfast lying on our backs
Because the shells were screeching overhead.
I bet a rasher to a loaf of bread
That Hull United would beat Halifax
When Jimmy Stainthorpe played full-back instead
Of Billy Bradford. Ginger raised his head
And cursed, and took the bet, and dropt back dead.
We ate our breakfast lying on our backs
Because the shells were screeching overhead.

(above) A comrade helping a wounded British soldier during the Battle of Mons, August 1914. The First World War was a war of guns. In the course of the fighting in France, the British alone fired over 170 million shells. In one fourteen-day battle in 1917, four million of them were fired at a cost of £22 million.

(right) We are making a new world, a painting by Paul Nash, 1917. Nash was a young artist, commissioned to record the war by the Imperial War Museum in London. Appalled by what he saw in France, he wrote,

'No glimmer of God's hand is seen anywhere. Sunset and sunrise are ... mockeries to man, only the black rain out of the bruised and swollen clouds all through the bitter black night is fit atmosphere in such a land. The rain drives on, the stinking mud becomes more evilly yellow, the shell holes fill up with green-white water, the roads and tracks are covered in inches of slime, the black dying trees ooze and sweat and the shells never cease ...'

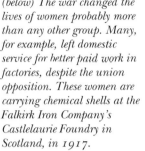

(left) Badges like this were sold on the streets at home.

(below) The war changed the lives of women probably more than any other group. Many, for example, left domestic service for better paid work in factories, despite the union opposition. These women are carrying chemical shells at the Falkirk Iron Company's Castlelaurie Foundry in Scotland, in 1917.

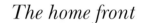

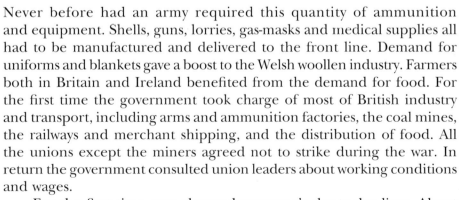

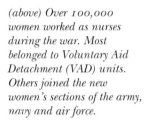

(above) Over 100,000 women worked as nurses during the war. Most belonged to Voluntary Aid Detachment (VAD) units. Others joined the new women's sections of the army, navy and air force.

The home front

Never before had an army required this quantity of ammunition and equipment. Shells, guns, lorries, gas-masks and medical supplies all had to be manufactured and delivered to the front line. Demand for uniforms and blankets gave a boost to the Welsh woollen industry. Farmers both in Britain and Ireland benefited from the demand for food. For the first time the government took charge of most of British industry and transport, including arms and ammunition factories, the coal mines, the railways and merchant shipping, and the distribution of food. All the unions except the miners agreed not to strike during the war. In return the government consulted union leaders about working conditions and wages.

For the first time, war changed everyone's day-to-day lives. About 1500 civilians were killed by bombs dropped first by airships, later by aeroplanes. In Hartlepool 119 people were killed in a raid by German airships in December 1914. One family recorded how they made immediate plans to move inland. The headmaster of the local school recorded the shelling of the school in his log book, the town was bombarded by German ships of war between 8 and 9 a.m ... the room at the south end of the school was filled with debris, a large portion of the ceiling having fallen ... One of the scholars – Bertie Young – was struck behind the ear by a piece of shell and died the same day.

For many women, life changed completely. To release men for the forces, they ran trams and buses, stoked furnaces, drove cranes, built ships and made ammunition.

Hardly a family was left untouched by the death or injury of a relative at the front. In battle after battle army generals ordered waves of men out of their trenches and 'over the top' in an attempt to overwhelm the enemy's positions, only for them to be mown down by the deadly fire of machine guns. At the Battle of the Somme in 1916, there were 420,000 British casualties, 60,000 of them, including 21,000 killed, on the first day alone. At Passchendaele a year later 324,000 men were killed or wounded.

The cover of an issue of the magazine Irish Life, *with a report of the events of the Easter Rising. Most of the damage to buildings was caused by British shells.*

The Easter Rising

In Ireland, after the first enthusiasm for recruitment had died away, many began to see the war as a 'British' war. A small group of Irish nationalists, who believed Ireland would only become a republic by force, welcomed the war as an opportunity. Although they had little support, a group led by the Irish Republican Brotherhood laid their plans for rebellion. Some 1600 armed volunteers, commanded by Patrick Pearse, occupied sites in central Dublin on Easter Monday, 24 April 1916. From his headquarters in the General Post Office, Pearse proclaimed Ireland a republic. The British immediately sent troops to Dublin. Six days later, with most of the area wrecked by artillery, Pearse ordered his volunteers to surrender. About 500 people had been killed, of whom 318 were civilians and over 2000 other civilians were wounded.

At first, most Irish people were angry with the rebels for causing unnecessary bloodshed and destruction. Then Asquith gave General Maxwell, the British army commander, power to court martial and imprison people without trial. The British arrested over 3,500 people. Pearse and fourteen other leaders were executed by firing squad.

The rebels were now hailed as heroes by the Irish. In the House of Commons John Dillon, deputy leader of the Irish Party, warned MPs, 'You are letting loose a river of blood ... between two races who, after three hundred years of hatred and strife, we had nearly succeeded in bringing together'. Too late, Asquith gave orders to stop the executions; the British had provided the republican cause with martyrs and, in Irish eyes, were the enemy once again. Two years later, a small republican political party called Sinn Féin ('Ourselves Alone') won nearly all the parliamentary seats in southern Ireland.

The German submarine campaign caused food shortages in Britain. At first the government tried to persuade people to eat less. Later it used a system of rationing, to control the amount of food people could buy.

The road to victory

In the war against Germany, British politicians expected a great naval victory, but it never happened. At first the German fleet stayed in port. In 1916 it ventured into the North Sea to be met by the British. The Battle of Jutland left neither side victorious but with the British still in command of the sea. For, while the British suffered the greater losses, the German fleet returned to port where it remained for the rest of the war.

Instead the German admirals conducted a new kind of naval warfare. They used submarines to blow up British merchant ships carrying food and raw materials. Knowing that American ships were also carrying vital supplies to Britain, the Germans attacked those too. In March 1917 Lloyd George, who had replaced Asquith as Prime Minister in 1916, publicly urged the United States to join the war,

> the French and British are buoyed with the knowledge that the great Republic of the West will neglect no effort which can hasten its troops and ships to Europe. In war time ... it is impossible to exaggerate the importance of getting American reinforcements across.

A month later the Americans were on their way.

At last it came to an end; soldiers were told 'stand fast on the line reached at 11 a.m. on 11 November 1918'. Germany had been defeated partly because she was exhausted, partly as a result of Allied victories in France, and partly because of American help. In London crowds outside Buckingham Palace yelled for the king, and sang hymns and then songs from the war. In Wales, Robert Graves, a writer and poet in the army, described how, 'The news sent me out walking alone ... cursing and sobbing and thinking of the dead.'

CHAPTER 3

'Peace in our time'

❖

When the Great War ended in 1918 the shadow of the 750,000 young British dead lay across the land. In their honour, and for the sake of the 2.5 million wounded and the thousands of returning servicemen and women, it did not seem too much to expect that the country which had united in the effort to fight the war should now unite in an effort to create a better society.

As Prime Minister at the head of a 'coalition government' of all parties, Lloyd George had worked hard to win the war. In the general election in December 1918, he was rewarded by an enormous vote of confidence. For the first time the voters included women as, during the war, Britain took a large but still not final step towards becoming a full democracy. In 1914 no women, and only fifty-eight per cent of adult men, were entitled to vote. In 1918 the government decided to reward those who had fought for their country, and enfranchised all men over twenty-one and married women over thirty. Only six million women qualified.

After the First World War memorials were put up in every town and village, to commemorate those who died. This one is in the village of Bellingham in Northumberland. In 1920 the Cenotaph, designed by Sir Edwin Lutyens, was put up in Whitehall, London, as a national memorial. Today these memorials are still the focus of a ceremony involving two minutes' silence, held every year on the Sunday closest to 11 November, Armistice Day, when the fighting ceased in 1918.

Children learning about shopping in an elementary school in Bradford in 1925. The Education Act of 1918 made elementary schools free, but secondary schools remained fee-paying.

Reform and disappointment

For a brief two years, as the government introduced reforms which affected everyday life, it appeared that this dream might come true. All children aged between five and fourteen had free full-time schooling in elementary schools, and the government gave money to help councils build new homes. A new Ministry of Health looked after public health; but in 1919 an influenza epidemic killed 150,000 people, a reminder that health insurance covered only the family wage earner. Everyone else still had to pay to see a doctor.

With the war over, the coal, steel and munitions industries needed fewer workers, and the government had to try to pay back enormous sums of borrowed money. The programme of social reform was taken no further. On the streets, the sight of ex-servicemen unable to find jobs or homes suggested that Lloyd George's ambition to make Britain 'a fit country for heroes to live in' was already in difficulties.

Many of the reasons for the divisions in the country in 1914, divided it still. Miners and railway workers went on strike, and at one time even the police stopped work. *The Times* described the situation as a war which 'like the war with Germany, must be a fight to the finish'. Lloyd George ordered soldiers on to the streets to keep order and by doing so lost his reputation as the workers' friend. In 1922 the Conservatives won the general election and Andrew Bonar Law became the new Prime Minister.

An old lady being overtaken by 'new women' wearing the latest fashions. It was becoming acceptable for women to drive cars and go out alone.

New women?

With the war over, young people, especially from better-off families, wanted more fun out of life and more freedom in fashion and behaviour. The change for many women, in particular, was dramatic. In the 1920s the pre-war practice of wearing very tight corsets ended and shorter skirts and hairstyles came into fashion. 'New women', as they were called, used make-up and smoked in public for the first time. A ballroom dancing craze swept towns and cities and couples could go to the new *palais-de-danse* halls. The Charleston was a popular new dance to jazz music.

For other women life simply went back to normal. The men returned from the forces to their old jobs. According to the *Southampton Times* in 1919,

A photograph of the writer Virginia Woolf taken in 1902. In the 1920s many writers experimented with new ways of expressing themselves, trying to make sense of a world shattered by war. In his novel Ulysses *(1922) the Irish writer James Joyce found ways of revealing the unspoken thoughts and feelings of his characters without describing them directly to the reader. Virginia Woolf used similar methods in her novels* Mrs Dalloway *(1925),* To the Lighthouse *(1925) and others.*

> women still have not brought themselves to realize that factory work, with the money paid for it during the war, will not be possible again ... women who left domestic service to enter the factory are now required to return to the pots and pans.

Yet things could never be quite the same. In Oxfordshire, Mont Abbott remembered how life changed for women in the country:

> Used to doing the men's work while they were away, the womenfolk took on more and more now we was at peace. We even had women bellringers, and women in the choir, and – the biggest revolution of all – the Women's Institute.

In the 1920s Parliament gradually improved women's rights, giving them better maternity benefits, divorce on the same grounds as men, equal guardianship rights to children and the right to hold and dispose of property on the same terms as men.

New states in Ireland

In the 1918 general election Sinn Féin won seventy-three seats outside the six northern counties of Ulster, while the Irish Party which argued for Home Rule won only six. Refusing to go to Westminster, the Sinn Féin representatives set up the Dáil Éireann in Dublin, calling it the parliament of the Irish Republic. The Irish Volunteers, led by Michael Collins, renamed themselves the Irish Republican Army (IRA) and began to attack the Royal Irish Constabulary (RIC) and the British army.

Protestants in Ulster remained committed to union with the United Kingdom. As Lloyd George needed their votes in the House of Commons, any decision about Ireland's future had to be acceptable to them. In 1920 he created two Home Rule governments, one for Ulster and the other for the rest of the country. In 1921 a Unionist government was elected to run the new state of Northern Ireland.

In the south, as Michael Collins's 'flying columns' attacked the RIC and troops, the British sent over ex-soldiers as additional police. Known as Black and Tans because their uniform was a mixture of army khaki and the black-green worn by the police, they made ruthless attacks on people and their homes in revenge for IRA attacks. In July 1921 both sides agreed a truce in what republicans now called the 'War of Independence'. Lloyd George proposed a treaty which offered the twenty-six southern counties of Ireland dominion status within the British Empire, as the Irish Free State. This meant that the new state would have the freedom to make its own laws but would also acknowledge the British monarch as head and follow the British government's foreign policy.

A market square in County Cork. Nearly three quarters of the population of the Irish Free State lived in the countryside, and earned a living by farming.

In December 1921 representatives of the Dáil reluctantly signed the Treaty. Back in Dublin the Dáil split. Eamon de Valera, President of the unofficial Irish Republic, condemned the Treaty as a betrayal of the ideals for which so many had fought. The pro-Treaty group argued that it was the best they could achieve without further war against the British. The new state was plunged into a bloody civil war. A year later, the pro-Treaty forces had won.

At first de Valera refused to recognize the Free State, but in 1926 he formed a new party, Fianna Fáil ('Warriors of Ireland'), to campaign in the general election for the Dáil the following year. To take his seat, he had to sign an oath of allegiance to the British monarch. 'I am prepared to put my name down in this book in order to get into the Dáil,' he said, 'but it has no other significance … You must remember I am taking no oath'.

'Give peace in our time, O Lord'

In the election of 1924 Labour won, benefiting from the support of thousands of working class people who now had the vote. Thus it was a Scottish politician, the Labour leader Ramsay MacDonald, whom George V invited to form a government. It was a dramatic moment. No one had expected the Labour Party to become so strong so soon.

Many feared that a Labour government would be dominated by trade unionists and socialists who would want the state to control the mines, railways and factories. But MacDonald steered a more moderate course. He was determined to stay in power, and he needed the support of the middle class voters. However, in the second general election in 1924 the Conservatives defeated Labour, and Stanley Baldwin became Prime Minister.

Baldwin's down-to-earth, pipe-smoking image was reassuring for the masses of people who wanted quiet lives after the turmoil of the war. When, in the House of the Commons in 1925, he asked all parties to echo his prayer, 'Give peace in our time, O Lord', he was talking about peace at home between the government and the trade unions; but within a year the country was plunged into conflict.

The trouble started in the coal industry. Mine owners, faced with less demand from abroad, reduced coal prices and asked the miners to accept longer hours and lower pay. In Durham and South Wales the owners proposed rates which

Many middle class volunteers appeared to enjoy themselves during the General Strike. Here they are putting barbed wire over the bonnet of a bus, to stop strikers getting at the engine. Still, they greeted the end with relief. Church services were held throughout the country to give thanks for the return of peace and unity. The strikers felt betrayed by the weakness of the TUC leaders who had given in.

were lower than those of 1914. The miners' leader, Arthur Cook, replied with the slogan, 'Not a minute on the day, not a penny off the pay', and the Trades Union Congress (TUC), a body founded in 1868 to which most trade unions belonged, supported him. The TUC warned Baldwin that if wage cuts went ahead, it would call a General Strike. The owners cut the rates and on Monday 3 May the strike began. Throughout the country nothing moved. There were no trains, trams or buses. Factories and foundries were empty. Pits lay silent.

Baldwin, however, had laid plans to run essential services if there was a strike. On the night of 2 May the government sent out a coded telegram saying 'Action'. Soon troops were taking over the work of dockers, miners and postmen. Middle class volunteers helped the police and drove buses, vans and even trains. Although there was no loss of life there was certainly violence. In Doncaster a crowd of around a thousand were charged by police with batons when they tried to stop traffic and eighty-four men received prison sentences. Strikers overturned buses in Glasgow and clashed with police in London, Preston, Hull, Middlesbrough and Liverpool.

A Labour Party election poster of 1929. This was the first election in which all women over twenty-one were entitled to vote. All parties tried to attract their votes. In 1919 Nancy Astor had become the first woman MP to take her seat. By 1923 there were only twenty-three women MPs.

The country was clearly split. The issue, said Baldwin, was who governed Britain: the government or the trade unions? This question also worried the TUC leaders who had called the strike to support the miners, not to overthrow an elected government. Frightened by what might happen if the strike continued, they called it off after nine days, leaving the miners to fight on alone. In November they too gave up and returned to work for lower pay, beaten by cold weather, hunger and lack of money.

Depression and the National Government

When the General Strike was over the problems of British industry remained. More workers lost their jobs, and Britain still had to pay off her war debts. When, in the general election of 1929, the voters elected a second Labour government with MacDonald again as Prime Minister, it was overtaken by events beyond its control. In the same year a financial crisis in the USA, known as the Wall Street Crash, forced many American banks to close and thousands of individuals and firms were ruined.

The crash soon affected the rest of the world, as Americans stopped buying from abroad. In Britain factories laid off workers and by 1931 there were nearly three million unemployed. Labour ministers disagreed about what to do and, in 1931, most of them resigned. Ramsay MacDonald proposed a National Government of all parties to cope with the crisis and, to everyone's surprise, he remained Prime Minister, although most of his ministers were Conservatives.

Two Britains

In the 1920s and 1930s the lives of those who worked in new industries were very different from those whose work depended on the old pre-war heavy industries of mining, shipbuilding, steel and railways. The new industries were based on technology and innovation, and used electricity instead of steam. They included electrical and car companies set up before the war, which now flourished in the midlands and the south of England. Other firms produced aeroplanes, chemicals, processed food and new materials such as plastics, and artificial fibres such as rayon.

With no need to be near coalfields the new factories were built on pleasant sites among green fields on the edges of towns. The Hoover factory was built in 1931 on Western Avenue in Perivale, London. The manufacturers of new consumer products such as electrical goods and cars liked their factories to be near London, which was their main market. This factory is a good example of the new 'art deco' style of architecture and design in the 1930s.

The old industries, mainly in the north of England, in south Wales, Scotland and Northern Ireland, did not prosper. The USA, Germany and Japan had already begun to use the latest inventions in their coal mines and steel works. These needed fewer workers, which made their products cheaper than Britain's. British manufacturers made no such changes. During the war home demand for coal, steel, iron and cloth had increased but Britain's competitors took advantage of the fighting to supply these materials to Britain's foreign customers. After the war British manufacturers found their foreign markets had gone, and there was less demand at home. The Britain of the old industries, once the heart of the country's nineteenth-century prosperity, fell into decay.

In the countryside farmers faced similar problems. They had done well during the war, supplying the extra food needed. When the slump came they also suffered, as cheap foreign food flooded in again. British farmers could not compete. Unlike foreign producers they had failed to buy new machinery and so the cost of British food was much higher. In Enstone, Mont Abbott remembered how many were forced to ask for Parish Relief when their wartime wages were cut,

> None of us was classed as heroes for long. The Agricultural Wages Board was set up to standardize farm wages, and straightaway cut the top wartime wages from forty-five to twenty-five bob.

Decaying Britain

A typical main meal for this unemployed worker and his family was boiled fish, dry bread and tea. They lived in this room, two other half-rooms and a small kitchen.

Visiting industrial areas of the north in 1936, the writer, George Orwell, described a 'monstrous scenery of slagheaps, chimneys, piled scrap iron, paths of cindery mud crisscrossed by the prints of clogs'. Behind this bleak landscape lay a human tragedy. Over two million people were out of work in 1921, and almost three million in the worst year, 1932. Most lived in the old industrial areas. Having no job meant little money to keep a family fed and healthy. Adults and children went hungry, wore old clothes and boots (sometimes no boots at all) and could not afford to buy medicines or see a doctor.

The depression of the 1930s made existing problems worse. By 1934 sixty-eight per cent of the workforce in the northern town of Jarrow was unemployed, sixty-two per cent in Merthyr Tydfil. In Aberdeen a woman remembered how,

> Most of the people along the street was unemployed, looking for jobs. When the snow came on they used to queue the whole night to try to get a job in the snow … and the foreman came out and said, 'You, and you, and you.' Frozen with cold they'd stand – and yet they'd say the unemployed was lazy.

Scottish hunger marchers on their way to London. They were protesting against the fact that their families' incomes and possessions were taken into account when they applied for unemployment benefit.

Throughout the 1920s and 1930s people living in the depressed areas went on hunger marches to London to draw attention to their desperate situation. On the Jarrow Crusade of 1936 two hundred marchers were given food and shelter by well-wishers.

Prosperous Britain

In the midlands and south of England, life was less bleak. Only about six per cent of the workforce had no job in the 1930s. The scientists, engineers and technicians working in the new industries earned high wages and could buy their own homes. Rows of semi-detached houses sprang up on large estates built on the outskirts of towns near their factories. These were the new suburbs, far larger than any built before the war. In this prosperous part of Britain people had money to spend on luxury goods and entertainment. In 1934 one British writer, J. B. Priestley, described it as a world of,

> filling [petrol] stations and factories that look like exhibition buildings, of giant cinemas and dance halls and cafés, bungalows with tiny garages, cocktail bars, Woolworths, motor coaches, wireless, hiking, factory girls looking like actresses, greyhound racing and dirt tracks, swimming pools, and everything given away for cigarette coupons.

A room interior showing the styles of the 1930s.

(left) A British radio, made in 1932, out of a new material called bakelite. Everyone who could afford one bought a wireless, as it was called then. In 1933 George V used radio to broadcast a Christmas Day message for the first time.

(above) A couple cleaning their car outside a typical suburban semi-detached house. The car was an important sign both of their prosperity and of their new freedom to get about. It was not used to get to work, but for weekend trips and holidays.

Getting by

Thousands of people all over Europe had no work, and in some places despair turned into violence. In Italy and Germany dictators who promised to put things right won votes. In Italy, in 1922, Mussolini became head of the government and in 1933 in Germany Hitler and his National Socialist (or Nazi) Party came to power. The Nazis looked for people to blame for Germany's troubles after the First World War. They managed to turn most people against the German Jews, and made laws that took away their rights.

In Britain, although many people were very poor while others were obviously well off, there was little support for violent attempts to overthrow the government. Only a few thousand people supported the unsuccessful British Union of Fascists, or 'Blackshirts', founded by Sir Oswald Mosley, a man who admired Mussolini and Hitler. Most people were hostile when Mosley tried to stir up anti-Jewish feeling in Britain. The nation which was governed by MacDonald's National Government was certainly divided, but it did not break up. Most poor families appeared more concerned to stay respectable and 'get by' than to attack those who were better off. As one East End Londoner put it in 1933,

We are happy in our own little world, and we know how to get along. Ma over her fish and chips is happier than many a rich lady at her banquet. And we know how to work things out in our own little world so that we get along some way.

A poster of 1924 to persuade women living in the suburbs to use the Underground to go shopping in central London. As today, there were 'rush hours' in the morning and evening, when people travelled to and from work.

Sport was very popular in the 1920s and 1930s, and the FA Cup final became an important national event. In 1923 it was played at Wembley Stadium for the first time. In this photograph, taken at the 1932 FA Cup Final, Newcastle United have just beaten Arsenal.

EAST COAST JOYS
travel by L·N·E·R
TO THE DRIER SIDE OF BRITAIN

Hiking became a popular pastime in the 1930s.

A poster for the British première of the Hollywood film Gone with the Wind. *The British actress Vivien Leigh won an Oscar for her performance. In the 1930s filmstars were heroes and heroines, and Hollywood set the fashions.*

Some living in the old industrial areas saw a brighter future in southern England. A steady flow of younger people left their families and friends and moved south to a new life where there might be jobs.

The majority who did not move 'got by' in various ways. The writer George Orwell reckoned that people bought cheap luxuries to make life bearable, so that,

> It is quite likely that fish and chips, art-silk [artificial silk] stockings, tinned salmon, cut-price chocolate …, the movies, the radio, strong tea and the football coupons have between them averted revolution.

The cinema was popular with people from all backgrounds. 'Once a week we go to the pictures', said a Lancashire woman in 1932. 'It's a big slice out of the week's money, but for me it's pictures or going mad. I forget my troubles.' For some the radio also offered entertainment. The British Broadcasting Company, set up in 1922, became the British Broadcasting Corporation in 1926.

In the splendour of wide screen, 70mm. and full stereophonic sound!

DAVID O. SELZNICK'S PRODUCTION OF MARGARET MITCHELL'S

"GONE WITH THE WIND"

CLARK GABLE
VIVIEN LEIGH
LESLIE HOWARD OLIVIA de HAVILLAND

Winner of Ten Academy Awards

A SELZNICK INTERNATIONAL PICTURE · VICTOR FLEMING · SIDNEY HOWARD · METRO-GOLDWYN-MAYER INC. · MAX STEINER   METROCOLOR

'The woman I love'

Despite the great divisions in society in the 1920s and the 1930s the British were generally patriotic people, and the monarchy was popular. There were great celebrations in 1935 for George V's Silver Jubilee. In 1936 Edward, the Prince of Wales, visited many depressed areas and appeared to be genuinely concerned about the problems facing jobless people. 'Something ought to be done to find these people employment', he said on a visit to South Wales. Yet it was he who plunged the monarchy into crisis.

In 1936 his father died and he became Edward VIII; but he was never crowned. He shocked the nation by wishing to marry Wallis Simpson, an American woman who had been twice-married and once divorced. The Church of England opposed divorce and, as monarch, Edward VIII was head of the Church. The Archbishop of Canterbury and Baldwin, the Prime Minister, opposed him. Baldwin told Edward that he had to choose between Mrs Simpson and the throne. The king agonized and then announced his decision to give up the throne. In his abdication speech on the radio he told the nation, 'I cannot discharge my duties as king without the help and support of the woman I love'. The new king, George VI (1936–1952), was Edward's brother. Gradually, with the help of his popular wife, Queen Elizabeth, he managed to restore the respect which the monarchy had lost as a result of Edward's abdication.

'The Empire was all around us', according to a writer who was a boy in the 1930s. Cigarette cards, children's annuals and biscuit tins carried pictures and stories about it, while school history textbooks described how the empire had been built up since Tudor times, and told of the deeds of the explorers, sailors, soldiers and missionaries who had made this possible.

Empire and dominions

The largest area on every map in every school was coloured red, and every child knew that red meant the British Empire. Most people were proud of the empire, and its size increased when the Treaty of Versailles gave Britain several former German colonies and territories lost by Turkey.

During the First World War India had made a huge contribution to the war effort, and Indian leaders now demanded that in return India should become self-governing. Whether or not Britain wanted to grant their demands the truth was that she could no longer afford to run an empire. Britain agreed to grant eventual self-government to India, but refused to say when. In India Mohandas

A poster celebrating the 60th anniversary of the confederation of Canada. In 1867 the separate Provinces of Ontario, Quebec, New Brunswick and Nova Scotia had been united to form the self-governing Dominion of Canada. Other provinces joined later.

Gandhi (known as Mahatma, meaning 'great soul') launched a series of non-violent civil disobedience campaigns against British rule. In 1935 Parliament eventually passed the Government of India Act, which arranged for Indian ministers to run the eleven provinces of India. The British still ran the central government, and there was no mention of eventual full independence.

The dominions – Canada, South Africa, Australia and New Zealand – also expected some reward for their sacrifices in the First World War. Although they were self-governing, they were still expected to follow British foreign policy and Britain did not treat them as her equals as they felt she should. In 1931, as a result of their demands, Parliament passed the Statute of Westminster. This recognized the dominions' complete independence from Britain and said that in future Britain and the dominions were to be equal members of an organization to be known as the British Commonwealth.

Under the treaty of 1922 the Irish Free State had also become a dominion. In 1932, when de Valera's party, Fianna Fáil, won a general election, he became head of the Free State government and set about dismantling the treaty. Although he abolished the oath of allegiance and removed the British monarch as head of state, the Free State remained a member of the British Commonwealth.

Faraway countries

In 1919 Allied leaders were determined to prevent the terrors of the First World War ever happening again. First they tried to make sure that Germany should never again be able to fight. In the peace treaty, signed at Versailles, they forced Germany to give land to other countries, pay money and raw materials to the victors, to cut down her armed forces and promise never to increase them again. Then, in 1920, they set up the League of Nations. It had fifty-eight members. Hoping to keep world peace, they undertook to protect each other against aggressors. At first the League had some successes, but when in 1931 Japan took over a province of China called Manchuria, and in 1935 Italy invaded the East African kingdom of Ethiopia, the League did little to stop them.

In Germany the leader of the Nazi party, Adolf Hitler, now realized that other countries were unlikely to cause trouble if he carried out his plans to recover the land which Germany had lost in 1919. He defied the terms of the Treaty of Versailles by building up his armed forces and then, in 1936, sent troops into the Rhineland, a German territory along the river Rhine which was supposed to be free of German armed forces.

Hitler gambled on the weakness of the League of Nations, and won. To the leaders of France and Britain it seemed reasonable for Germany to re-occupy her own territory, as long as other countries were not threatened, and Hitler insisted that there was no threat. Winston Churchill spoke only for a few when he argued that to give in to dictators would only make them more aggressive and that Hitler should be stopped straight away. This policy of appeasement, he warned, would encourage Hitler to seize more territory. His advice was ignored.

A peace march. In the early 1930s most British people were very anxious to avoid war. In 1934 Lord Cecil, the President of the League of Nations, organized a nationwide 'peace ballot'. Eleven million people (nearly half the adult population) said they supported the League; 10 million were in favour of disarmament.

In 1938 Hitler gambled again. As German troops marched into Austria he claimed that, as a German-speaking area, it should be part of Germany. He then demanded another German-speaking area – the Sudetenland in Czechoslovakia. The Czechs refused to hand it over and appealed to their allies for help. Once again Europe seemed to be on the brink of war. Neville Chamberlain, who had succeeded Baldwin as Prime Minister in 1937, flew to Germany to meet Hitler who assured him that the Sudetenland was the final piece of land he wanted.

In September 1938 Chamberlain and the leaders of France and Italy met Hitler in Munich to resolve the matter. They agreed that the Czechs should hand over the Sudetenland to Germany. Before he left for Munich Chamberlain had broadcast to the British nation, saying,

> How horrible, fantastic, incredible it is that we should be digging trenches and trying on gas-masks here because of a quarrel in a faraway country between people of whom we know nothing.

Rescuing a victim of the Blitz in London, 1940. After the Battle of Britain, German bombers continued to pound British cities. Ports and major cities such as Plymouth, Bristol, Belfast, Glasgow, Liverpool, Manchester, Coventry, Swansea and Hull were among the many targets, as well as London. In retaliation the RAF was sent on massive (and, many now feel, unnecessarily destructive and brutal) raids against civilians in German cities.

toil, tears and sweat,' he told MPs as the Allied armies retreated before the German advance.

In only two weeks the German army pushed back the British forces to the beaches of Dunkirk on the French coast. It was a humiliating defeat, but the British rescued their pride by the daring of their escape. In a week-long operation Royal Navy and merchant ships, and hundreds of pleasure boats, crossed the Channel and successfully rescued 300,000 troops (a third of whom were French). By 3 June 1940 almost the entire British army was home. If the Germans invaded, Churchill promised, 'We shall fight on the beaches, we shall fight on the landing grounds, we shall fight in the fields and in the streets'.

Within three weeks the Germans had entered Paris. France surrendered and Britain stood alone against Germany. On the radio the Labour MP, Ernest Bevin, now Minister of Labour, told the nation,

> Everyone in the land is a soldier for liberty. We must regard ourselves as one army … Hitler's success will be brought to nought, and the name of Britain will go down in history, not as a great imperialist nation but as a marvellous people in a wonderful island, that stood at a critical moment in the world's history between tyranny and liberty and won.

A million men answered an appeal for part-time soldiers to help defend the country against invasion; but Hitler was not yet ready. Instead he launched the air attack which everyone feared, planning first to wipe out Britain's airforce and then to bombard her cities. In the hot summer of 1940 the Royal Air Force and the German Luftwaffe fought the decisive Battle of Britain in the skies over southern England.

In August the Luftwaffe launched air-raids on airfields using up to a thousand bombers at a time. In September the attack switched to London. This was the Blitz (a word created from the German *blitzkrieg*, meaning 'lightning war'). Between 300 and 600 Londoners were killed each day, and thousands more were injured. The RAF, almost defeated at one point, managed to fight on. By October the Luftwaffe was beaten. The Germans continued to bomb Britain, but without control of the air Hitler could no longer hope to invade.

Women building a barrage balloon in 1942. By 1943 forty per cent of all the workers in the aircraft industry were female. By 1944 there were 500,000 women in the services, 200,000 in the Women's Land Army and over 300,000 doing work for the government in the civil service.

The home front

The war involved the whole population of the United Kingdom. All men aged between nineteen (later eighteen) and forty-one were called up to fight. Many women volunteered and in 1941 all unmarried women between twenty and thirty were conscripted. They could choose to join the women's section of one of the armed forces (although they were not allowed to fight) or the Women's Land Army, which worked on farms to help produce food. They could also work in a factory. One girl from Newcastle was already working in a munitions factory when she was about fifteen, then she decided to join the Land Army.

We had a twelve hour journey from Newcastle on the train and the farmer was waiting for us at Shepton Mallet [in Somerset]... When we got to the hostel ...we were starving and shattered and cold. ...when we saw the iron bunks, I thought, 'God no, I want to go home.'

Food was in short supply from the start. Rationing began in 1940, first for sugar, butter, cheese and bacon, then for tea, fats and margarine. The government told people to 'Dig for Victory' and grow as much of their own fruit and vegetables as they could. In 1941 clothes were rationed and everyone was encouraged to 'Make Do and Mend', so that old clothes would last as long as possible. One woman remembered trying to look her best for an interview for a job,

POTATOES feed without fattening and give you *ENERGY*

My mother had made me a costume, a kind of suit made out of bombed-out shop material ... she'd also made a pink blouse out of an old dress. I had no clothes coupons to buy anything new, and ... none to buy stockings.

(left) In 1943 the fashion designer Norman Hartnell launched his 'utility look'. The clothes were simple, practical and used as little material as possible.

(above) Posters like this one were produced by the Ministry of Food, to encourage people to eat healthily.

towards Germany. On 15 April 1945 British troops liberated the concentration camp at Belsen, one of several where the Germans had imprisoned and murdered millions of Jews in appalling conditions. Fifteen days later Hitler committed suicide in Berlin, and on 8 May the British people celebrated VE (Victory in Europe) Day. The following day General Montgomery received the Germans' unconditional surrender. The war in Europe was over.

VE Day celebration in London. A man from a mining village in South Wales, who was a boy on VE Day, later recalled, 'that was a beanfeast, we had a marvellous celebration down at the Salvation Army hall. Food suddenly appeared that we'd never even seen. I think a lot of it had been hoarded, and was suddenly unearthed; some of the tins were rusty by the look of them. I can remember that night walking up to Cross Keys, which was the next village, and celebrating on the bandstand.'

In the Far East the fighting continued for another three months, as the retreating Japanese offered fierce resistance. President Truman of the USA wanted to end the war with as little cost to American lives as possible. He therefore decided to use a secret weapon which had been developed in the USA during the war, with the help of British scientists. In August 1945 American planes dropped atomic bombs on the Japanese cities of Hiroshima and Nagasaki. Little remained of either city. Nearly 150,000 people were killed. The cloud rising up from the explosion looked, said a British observer, 'as though it were some horrible form of life'. A week later Japan surrendered. VJ (Victory in Japan) Day was on 15 August 1945. In Scotland the *Dalkeith Advertiser* recorded the words of the Provost of Dalkeith at the celebrations,

It has cost the Allied Nations six million men, dead and wounded … let us for a moment think of the price we have paid and also think for a few seconds of the fathers and mothers who have given up their sons to make your revelry possible at all.

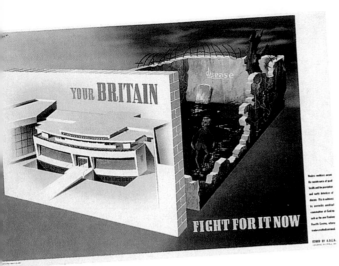

A poster of 1944 promising a new Britain after the war. A new Health Centre replaces a bombed-out building containing disease and death.

Fair shares for all

On the 'home front' 60,000 civilians had been killed in bombing raids and everyone had gone without to support the war effort. The government had promised 'Fair shares for all', and the work they did brought together people from different backgrounds. As the fighting went on, many politicians from all parties became convinced that once the war was over they really would have to build a new kind of society.

Plans for a better future began to take shape during the war itself. In 1942 Sir William Beveridge produced a report in which he described how five evil giants – Want (poverty), Disease (ill-health), Ignorance (lack of schooling), Squalor (poor housing) and Idleness (unemployment) – all blocked the way to a better Britain. He made proposals for abolishing for ever the kind of poverty in which so many people still lived. His ideas caught the public's imagination: 635,000 copies of the Report were sold.

Meanwhile R.A.Butler, the Minister of Education, planned to provide 'secondary education for all'. The 1944 Education Act required Local Authorities to provide meals, free milk and regular medical inspections. There were to be three types of school. Children who passed an exam at eleven went to grammar shools. For the others there were technical schools and secondary modern schools.

In May 1945, shortly after Germany's defeat but before the surrender of Japan, Labour ministers decided that the time was right for politics to return to normal. They resigned from Churchill's coalition, forcing him to call a general election. Which party could be entrusted with the task of creating a new and better society in a country exhausted by six years of fighting? To the surprise of many, the result was an overwhelming victory for Labour. Although grateful to Churchill for his leadership in war, many voters felt he was out of tune with their hopes for the peace. The new Labour Prime Minister was Clement Attlee. 'We are facing a new era', he said, 'Labour can deliver the goods'.

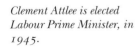

Clement Attlee is elected Labour Prime Minister, in 1945.

CHAPTER 5
Winds of change

❖

British hopes were high in the years immediately after the Second World War. Yet people still had to live with few luxuries because the country, having spent everything on the war, was now so poor. In 1947 the Prime Minister, Clement Attlee, told Parliament,'I have no easy words for the nation … I cannot say when we shall emerge into easier times'.

Bombing had destroyed many houses in the cities, and many families still lived in slums. People who had lost their homes were pleased to move into temporary homes like these, known as 'prefabs' (all the parts were prefabricated, made in advance, in factories). Over 100,000 were put up. Many lasted until the 1970s or even longer.

Hard times

In 1945 the government owed more than £3 billion to other countries, borrowed during the war. Somehow Britain had to start earning money again. This meant selling as much as possible to other countries, and buying as little as possible from them. The government decided to limit all imports except raw materials for industry. All food, clothes, petrol and many household items remained rationed. Recovery seemed agonizingly slow, but gradually life improved. By 1950 local councils had built one million council houses (all to a high standard with three bedrooms and an inside bathroom), but many more were needed.

In 1947 Billy Butlin re-opened his holiday camps and thousands of people flocked to enjoy cheap fun-packed weeks. 'Everything was so wonderful after the drabness of war … Butlins was the best thing that happened to ordinary people,' remembered one visitor. For the first time the government, through the new Arts Council of Great Britain, gave money to support professional arts organizations which put on exhibitions, plays, operas, ballets and concerts. The BBC offered three radio services instead of one: the Light Programme for popular entertainment, the Home Service for news and more serious programmes, and the Third Programme for classical music, drama and talks.

The cinema was as popular as ever after the war. Hollywood films drew large audiences, and so too did British films such as the Ealing Comedies or this film of Shakespeare's Henry V, made in 1944, with Laurence Olivier as both star and director.

Professional sport flourished. Huge crowds turned out to watch football and cricket. In 1947 a Great Britain football team beat the Rest of Europe 6–1 at Hampden Park in Glasgow, and the sporting hero of the year was Denis Compton, who played football for Arsenal and cricket for Middlesex and England. That summer he thrilled huge crowds by scoring four centuries in test matches against South Africa. The journalist, Neville Cardus, wrote,

> Never have I been so deeply touched on the cricket ground as I was this heavenly summer, when I went to Lord's to see a pale-faced crowd, existing on rations, the rocket bomb still in the ears of most folk – to see this worn, dowdy crowd watching Compton … There was no rationing in an innings by Compton.

Never again

Labour ministers planned to kill Beveridge's four evil giants (see page 45) and agreed with his idea that the state should be responsible for the welfare of its people 'from the cradle to the grave'. Their plans took shape in four Acts of Parliament, which together created the Welfare State. In return for a weekly payment everyone was entitled to free medical treatment from the new National Health Service, and to payments while they were ill or unemployed.

Labour also believed that important industries should be nationalized and run by the state for the public good. After 1945 they nationalized the privately-run coal mines, iron and steel industries, railways, road transport, and gas and electricity industries.

The National Health Service transformed the lives of most British people, who could not afford medical fees. The NHS provided free eye tests and spectacles, dental treatment and access to a doctor.

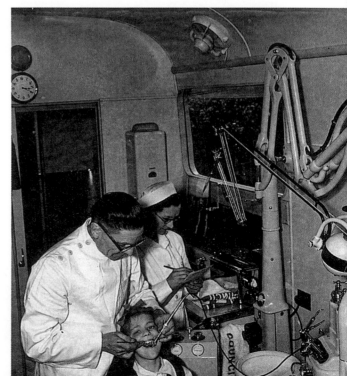

47

A COMMUNICATIONS REVOLUTION

Telecommunication uses electrical signals to send messages over long distances. The main forms are telephone, radio and television. Together they have revolutionized the lives of the British people in the twentieth century.

At the beginning of the century only wealthy people and businesses had a telephone. By the end there were millions of subscribers, who took it for granted that they could talk to someone else, almost anywhere in the world, at the touch of a button.

In the 1920s radio began to bring news and entertainment directly into people's homes. A Yorkshire woman remembered how, as a child,

> I went to my next-door neighbour's house and I saw this cone on the wall. And I went into my mother's and I said, 'Mother, Mrs Buckle's wall is singing'.

▲ *In the 1930s, when this advertisement was produced, private users began to out-number business users of the telephone. The telephone, perhaps more than any other invention, speeded up the pace of people's lives.*

▶ *Two typical telephones of the 1920s and 1930s.*

Television broadcasts started in 1936, but it was not until the 1950s that television became really popular. By 1969 nine out of ten households had a set, and a survey found that, on average, a quarter of each person's leisure time was spent watching television. Colour transmissions began in 1967, and screens became larger. By 1991 over 15 million households also had a video cassette recorder.

Meanwhile, in the 1980s mobile phones were invented, and also facsimile (fax) machines which could transmit and receive words and images along telephone lines. By the 1990s a combination of telephone, television, radio, satellite and computer technology made it possible for large amounts of information to be transmitted around the world in a few seconds.

△ *Television quickly changed the way people lived, and some people worried that it would have a bad effect on families. Because many families now ate 'TV dinners' in front of the television, they would not talk to each other. People might also stop reading books. But between 1945 and 1970 the number of books issued by public libraries nearly doubled.*

◁ *By the 1990s many homes, schools and businesses were linked up to an international computer network called the INTERNET. In 'cyber cafés' like this one, people could have a cup of coffee while exploring the amazing range of information on 'the net'.*

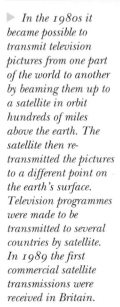

◁ *During the Second World War radio was an important source of entertainment and information. Nearly everyone listened to the news of the war on the radio in the evening. Radio was important for raising morale at home, and for creating a sense of national unity.*

▷ *In the 1980s it became possible to transmit television pictures from one part of the world to another by beaming them up to a satellite in orbit hundreds of miles above the earth. The satellite then re-transmitted the pictures to a different point on the earth's surface. Television programmes were made to be transmitted to several countries by satellite. In 1989 the first commercial satellite transmissions were received in Britain.*

The South Bank Exhibition buildings during the 1951 Festival of Britain. The Exhibition attracted nearly nine million visitors. In the centre of the picture is the Royal Festival Hall, today the centre of the South Bank Complex. To the right is the Dome of Discovery and, beyond that, the floodlit aluminium 'Skylon' described at the time as a 'luminous exclamation mark'. People joked that, like Britain, it had no visible means of support. Many of the exhibits confirmed Britain's strength in industries of the future such as aviation, electronics and communications.

The coronation of Queen Elizabeth II on 2 June 1953. The Coronation marked the real beginning of the television age. Thousands of families bought or hired televisions, and neighbours visited one another to watch. The commentator was Richard Dimbleby who had been a famous radio reporter during the war. He was able to explain to his viewers the meaning of every detail of a Coronation ceremony that had been used for a thousand years.

A new age?

In 1947 Herbert Morrison, the Deputy Prime Minister, told his Cabinet colleagues, 'We ought to do something jolly … We need something to give Britain a lift'. The result, in 1951, was the Festival of Britain, a deliberate echo of the Great Exhibition held a hundred years before. All over Britain events celebrated the achievements of Britain's artists, architects, scientists, engineers and designers. In London, on the bank of the River Thames, the centrepiece was the new building for the South Bank Exhibition. This told the story of Britain, her people and their achievements.

Two years later, following the death of George VI, the Coronation of Elizabeth II (1952–), made people talk of Britain entering a 'New Elizabethan Age'. At twenty-five Elizabeth II was the same age as her Tudor predecessor when she was crowned. When, on Coronation Day, the waiting crowds heard that two members of a British climbing expedition – a New Zealander, Edmund Hillary, and a Nepalese Sherpa, Tenzing Norgay – had for the first time reached the top of Mount Everest, it seemed that the New Elizabethans had already found their Francis Drake and Walter Raleigh.

Having it good

The new 'contemporary' style of room furnishing on display at the South Bank Exhibition, 1951. Fabrics and carpets often had bold geometric designs in bright colours.

Furniture often had thin legs and plastic or woven coverings. During the 1950s electric or central heating began to replace coal fires.

By 1951 people were tired of rationing and queues. In the general election of 1951, the Conservatives promised people more opportunity and freedom. They won and remained in power for the next thirteen years.

All the Conservative governments during this time (first with Sir Winston Churchill as Prime Minister, then Sir Anthony Eden, then Harold Macmillan and finally Sir Alec Douglas-Home) remained committed, like Labour, to the idea of the Welfare State and to maintaining a high level of employment. They spent money building new houses, hospitals and roads. People with jobs would spend their wages on goods, which would in turn benefit British industry.

These schemes meant that there were more new houses to rent and buy. New Towns, such as Stevenage, Cwmbran and Glenrothes expanded, and in the 1950s new labour-saving devices such as washing machines and vacuum cleaners became widely available again, as well as portable radios, record players and televisions. Many people had their first telephone installed. They also bought their first car, and buses and trains began to lose passengers.

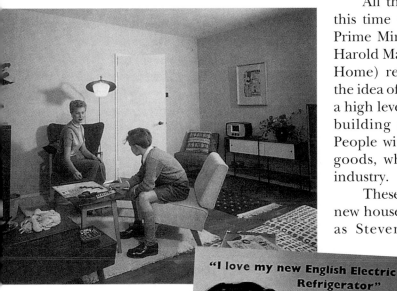

"I love my new English Electric Refrigerator"

'ENGLISH ELECTRIC'

In the 1950s many people could afford labour-saving gadgets for the first time.

At last, in 1954, food rationing ended. Already a new kind of shop, the supermarket, was beginning to appear in the high street. Between 1956 and 1961 eight hundred supermarkets were opened in Britain. By 1960 nearly one fifth of all households used a refrigerator, and shopping lists included frozen foods such as peas, chips, fish fingers and ice-cream. Even poorer families found they could afford the cheap prices of package holidays abroad. 'Most of our people have never had it so good', said the Prime Minister, Harold Macmillan, in 1957.

Teenagers

Young people probably had it best of all in the 1950s. Everyone could get a job, wages were rising and young adults living at home had spare earnings to spend. For the first time teenagers (the word was first used in the 1950s) had buying power, and entertainment and fashion changed to meet their demands.

In 1955 'Rock Around the Clock', played by the American band Bill Haley and the Comets, launched a new dance and music craze – rock 'n' roll. The music was fast, exciting and had a strong beat. Unlike formal ballroom dancing there were no set steps to learn. Young people could express themselves on the dance floor for the first time and had a new sense of power. As one of them put it in a letter to *The Times*, this was 'more than music',

It's a serious, outward and visible sign of a revolutionary change in the hearts of young people everywhere who are demanding the world be theirs. Rock 'n' roll is smashing and it's going to smash all the fuddy-duddy civilization to smithereens. Rock 'n' roll will change the world.

The first Expresso Bars in Britain opened in the 1950s. They quickly became a popular place for young people to meet casually to chat and listen to the latest records on the juke box. 'I remember how daring and rebellious I felt going to coffee bars,' one girl recalled. 'They were something new and different – places for teenagers to meet one another. The older generation was definitely excluded! We thought we were really "with it", so "cool" and in step with all the latest fashions. Those who didn't fit in, we simply wrote off as "squares".'

Adults, used to the discipline and self-sacrifice of the depression years and the war, began to wonder what the younger generation was coming to.

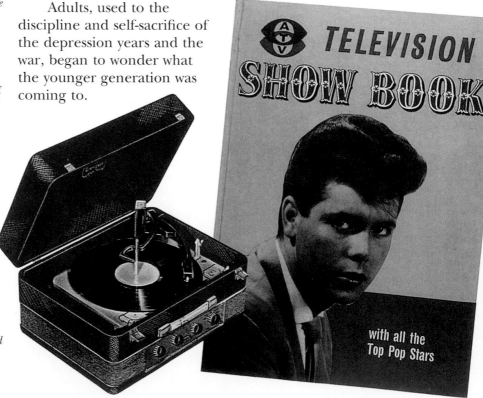

In the 1950s teenagers could buy newly-invented portable radios and record players, and magazines telling them about the latest stars of rock 'n' roll.

The Big Three

In 1945 Britain was one of the world's three great powers, known as the Big Three. The other two were the USA and the Soviet Union. Where the League of Nations had failed, they hoped the new United Nations Organization (UN) would succeed and bring about permanent world peace and co-operation between nations. Britain played an important part in setting up the UN and became one of the five permanent members of the Security Council, its main peacekeeping body.

To remain a great power Britain had to be strongly armed. In 1946 the government made the secret decision that Britain should build her own atomic bomb. The cost was immense, but Attlee and Ernest Bevin, the Foreign Secretary, were convinced that without it Britain would be tied to the USA and unable to act independently in world affairs.

At the same time Britain needed the USA. The communist Soviet Union, an important ally in the war, was now seen as a likely enemy. By 1946 Soviet troops had occupied most of Eastern Europe and half of Germany. In 1949 Britain, the USA and most of the other Western European states formed the North Atlantic Treaty Organization (NATO). Its purpose was to defend Western Europe against the Soviet Union.

A scene from John Osborne's play Look Back in Anger, *produced in London in 1956. This play changed the way many people thought about Britain. The central character, Jimmy Porter, attacked middle class British people, whom he saw as comfortable, boring, uncritical and too obedient to authority. The play came to be seen as representing the mood of the 'angry young man', rejecting the attitudes and beliefs of the older generation.*

Saying 'No' to Europe

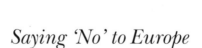

After the war, the countries of Western Europe had two main aims: to bring back prosperity, and to make it impossible for there ever to be another war in Europe. A French politician, Jean Monnet, proposed that the states of Europe should form a federation – a group of member states obeying a single, central government on important matters such as taxation, trade and defence, but keeping control of their own affairs on some other matters such as health and education.

Britain, however, had strong ties to the Empire and the Commonwealth, her main ally was the USA, and people remembered how they had been the only European country to resist Hitler effectively. The British felt separate from the rest of Europe and believed they had a worldwide role to play. Bevin wanted no part in a European union. Instead, he urged the Americans to give money (known as Marshall Aid) to help European countries recover from the war.

In 1950 Britain refused an offer to join the new European Coal and Steel Community, which placed the coal and steel industries of France, West Germany, Belgium, the Netherlands and Luxembourg under a common High Authority. Its success led its six members to create a 'common market'. This removed all customs barriers between them, and put a tax on all goods entering their group from outside. The Six hoped that as one big unit they would be able to rival countries such as the United States, and achieve a similar level of wealth and prosperity. In 1957 their representatives met in Rome to sign a treaty setting up the European Economic Community (EEC). Again Britain stood aside.

From Empire to Commonwealth

Attlee believed it was now the right time to give India its independence, and that Britain could keep the advantages of a close connection without the cost of government. In 1947 he appointed Lord Mountbatten to be the last Viceroy of India, with the power to arrange how Britain should hand over the government.

When Mountbatten arrived in India he faced a split between India's two main religious groups, the Hindus and the Muslims. Muslims demanded a separate state, to be called Pakistan, in those areas of India where Muslims were a majority. As violence between Hindus and Muslims increased it was clear that they could no longer live side by side in peace. On 14 August 1947 two new nations were born, Pakistan and India.

India, Pakistan and Ceylon (Sri Lanka), which became independent in 1948, all joined the British Commonwealth and kept close ties with Britain, as Attlee had hoped. Burma, made independent the year before, decided not to join, and the Irish Free State withdrew when it became the Republic of Ireland in 1949. Both felt that membership was too similar to the old colonial relationship with Britain.

Influenced by the Prime Minister of India, Jawaharlal Nehru, the Commonwealth began to change. India decided to become a republic, and no longer wished to recognize George VI as its monarch. The king agreed to take the new title of Head of the Commonwealth, and as long as members recognized this they did not have to keep the British monarch as their head of state.

Celebrations, and hope for the future, as Nigeria receives its independence, in 1960.

Britain's other colonies now demanded independence. The Gold Coast became the first African country to join the Commonwealth when it received its independence as Ghana in 1957. In 1960 the British Prime Minister, Harold Macmillan, shocked members of the all-white Parliament of South Africa when he told them that 'the wind of change is blowing through this Continent'.

By 1965 all British colonies in Africa, except for Southern Rhodesia (Zimbabwe), had become independent and joined the Commonwealth. Meanwhile the other members forced South Africa to leave the Commonwealth, because of its apartheid laws which kept black and white people separate at all times and placed political power in white hands. In 1961 South Africa became a republic.

From Big Three to Big Two

In 1956 Egypt decided to take control of the Suez Canal, which joined the Red Sea to the Mediterranean. It was owned by a French company, and was an important part of Britain's sea route to the Far East. When British and French troops occupied the Canal area, they were criticized at the UN, even by the USA and almost all the Commonwealth countries. Humiliated, Britain and France withdrew.

The Suez crisis showed that Britain was no longer rich enough to act alone in the world. The USA and the Soviet Union were the superpowers who really counted. The Big Three had become the Big Two.

The front page of the Daily Mirror *on 1 November 1956.*

The first Aldermaston March, on Easter Day 1958. During the 1950s many people became increasingly unhappy about Britain's involvement in hydrogen bomb tests and the government's decision to have nuclear weapons. Thousands of people joined the Campaign for Nuclear Disarmament (CND) when it was launched in 1958. Campaigners wanted Britain to give a lead to the world by giving up her nuclear weapons, even if no other country agreed to do the same. This was called 'unilateral nuclear disarmament'.

In 1962 a new magazine was published for the first time. Private Eye poked fun at politicians and exposed scandals. It began to change people's attitude from one of automatic respect for authority, to one that questioned the character, competence and values of the people in charge of Britain.

(below) In the 1960s high-rise housing estates, like this one in Sheffield, replaced many of the streets of back-to-back houses where most working class people in cities were used to living. The new flats had central heating, but the estates were often badly designed and residents were often lonely. Vandalism and crime flourished.

Supermac

The Conservatives won the general election in 1959. Britain appeared to be back on course under the guidance of the Prime Minister, Harold Macmillan. Most people felt they could afford the household goods flooding into the shops. The humiliation of Suez had been left behind. Good relations with the Americans seemed to be restored.

There was, many felt, a touch of wizardry about Macmillan. One cartoonist depicted him as 'Supermac', a cross between his real self and the popular cartoon figure Superman. Within four years, however, 'Supermac' had fallen to earth. By 1963, when he resigned as Conservative leader, Macmillan seemed to be out of touch. A series of scandals hit the government and the new Labour leader, Harold Wilson, made Macmillan look a failure.

What's wrong with Britain?

In the early 1960s Britain was at a turning point. When it was revealed that politicians and other well-known people used the services of prostitutes and took drugs, the news both entertained and shocked the public. Some said that the new prosperity had only made people more interested in buying goods than in caring about others. And the good times could not last. The British were beginning to buy more from abroad than they sold. Like a person, a country that spends more than it earns can quickly run into debt. France, Germany and Japan were obviously doing much better. The British began to realize that, although they had won the war, in economic terms they were losing the peace.

When the young John F. Kennedy became US President in 1961, he made it plain that, to the Americans, the 'special relationship' between Britain and the USA was no longer so important. In 1962 the retired US politician, Dean Acheson, said that Britain, 'has lost an empire and not yet found a role'.

Saying 'No' to Britain

Aware of Britain's weaknesses, Macmillan changed his views about the EEC and applied to join. As a leading nation in Europe, Britain might also recover her position in the world. However, the President of France, General de Gaulle, was strongly anti-American. The last thing he wanted was Britain, backed by the USA, challenging France for the leadership of Europe. In 1961 he voted against Britain's application.

Although most business leaders supported Macmillan, many people, including the Labour Party, feared that membership of the EEC would mean breaking important ties with the Commonwealth. In 1964 the new Labour leader, Harold Wilson, took a different view. Following Labour's victory in the general election, Wilson again applied for British membership of the EEC in 1967. Again De Gaulle said no.

Comfortable times

During the 1960s, despite worries about the state of British industry, most people were very much better off than ever before. There were plenty of jobs and spending on consumer goods continued. More people bought their own centrally heated homes. Do-It-Yourself home improvement became popular, encouraged by magazines such as *Homes and Gardens* and *Ideal Home.*

There was more time for leisure. In 1961 most manual workers had only two weeks holiday; by 1971 nearly all had three weeks, and some had four or more. According to a government survey in 1969, people spent a quarter of their spare time watching television, for nearly all households now had a television set, but they went to the cinema less often.

Watching sport on television increased. Football was the most popular sport. The BBC's 'Match of the Day' could attract ten million viewers on Saturday nights. In 1966 England won the World Cup, encouraging thousands of amateurs to play in their spare time. Meanwhile some of the professional players, who had been treated as ordinary workers and paid very low wages, became celebrities.

In 1962 a new Coventry Cathedral was consecrated, beside the ruins of the old one destroyed in 1940. The new building included work by British artists such as John Piper (the stained glass window) and Graham Sutherland (the tapestry behind the altar). The number of people going to church decreased through the century, but Christian beliefs remained important to many people.

MEDICINE

▶ *X-rays were first used in the 1890s, to see inside people's bodies. Since the rays can also destroy living tissue, they were soon being used to destroy cancerous growths. Modern scanners produce more detailed pictures of the body's interior, using very low doses of X-rays to reduce the risk to patients.*

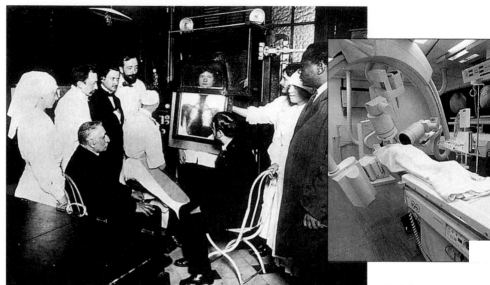

Improvements in medicine were among the few good things to result from the two world wars. After the First World War, for example, doctors learned how to carry out a successful transfusion of new blood into a patient, and scientists developed vaccines against typhus and tetanus, diseases which had caused death and sickness among the soldiers.

The greatest dream of doctors, however, was to find a substance that would destroy killer germs in soldiers' wounds, without also destroying the white blood cells which helped to fight those germs. In 1928 the breakthrough came, when Alexander Fleming, a Scottish researcher, discovered a substance that could do this. He called it penicillin. It was the most important medical discovery of the century so far, but it was not until the Second World War that scientists learned how to use the drug to cure patients.

The founding of the National Health Service (NHS) in 1948 brought free health care to all for the first time. In the second half of the century, advances in surgery have

▼ *A busy out-patients department in a London Hospital, 1949. Now that everyone could also visit a doctor or dentist, it became easier to inoculate people against serious diseases such as diphtheria or polio, so they were virtually wiped out.*

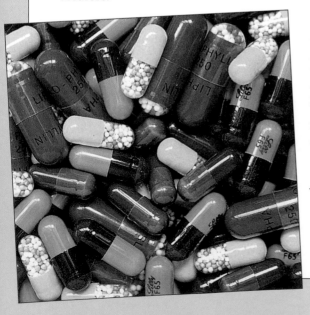

◀ *Since penicillin was first used, in the Second World War, other antibiotics (drugs which kill germs called bacteria) have saved millions of lives all* *over the world. Thousands more life-saving drugs have been developed, to treat both physical and mental illnesses.*

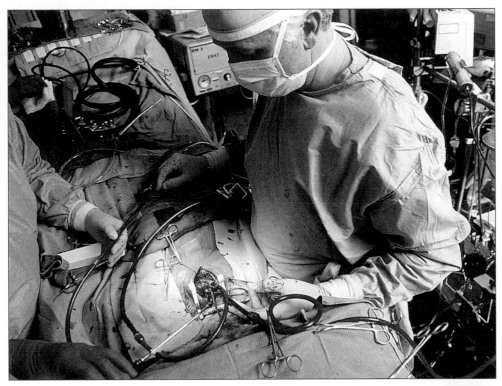

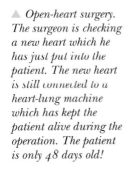

Open-heart surgery. The surgeon is checking a new heart which he has just put into the patient. The new heart is still connected to a heart-lung machine which has kept the patient alive during the operation. The patient is only 48 days old!

prolonged and improved people's lives. It has become possible to transplant organs such as a heart, lung or liver, from one person to another. Replacing damaged hip bones with artificial joints has become a fairly routine operation for the elderly, allowing them to walk with far less pain.

In 1972 the world's first 'test tube baby', Louise Brown, was born in Oldham, Greater Manchester, following years of research into ways of helping couples who could not conceive a baby. New operating and scanning techniques have revolutionized surgery. Enormous advances in our under-standing of our genes, the codes in our bodies that tell them how to grow, have led to research into curing inherited diseases. Meanwhile, there has been a growing interest in 'alternative medicine', techniques for curing illness that do not rely on drugs or surgery.

A laser beam being used in an eye operation. Lasers allow very small, precise cuts to be made. This causes the least possible damage to the surrounding tissues. Patients recover more quickly from these operations than from open surgery where knives are used.

In 1962 two British scientists, Crick and Watson, received a Nobel Prize for working out the structure of the DNA molecule, shown here. DNA is the basis of our genes, which contain the chemical codes that determine how our bodies are formed. Genes can have mistakes in them which cause disease. As genes are inherited, so are some diseases. Scientists may now be able to prevent this by replacing unhealthy genes with healthy ones.

The swinging sixties

In the 1960s Britain's young people were at the centre of a fashion revolution which burst on to the high streets. It was led by young designers like Mary Quant, who in 1955 had opened her first shop in King's Road, in London. They designed colourful, informal, cheap clothes, and it was Mary Quant who introduced mini-skirts and tights. Joy James, who was twelve in 1960, remembered, 'As a nearly-teenager I was awkwardly weighed down with stockings and suspender-belts, vests and tummy-flattening girdles. The 1960s brought Freedom!'

Sixties fashions changed with bewildering speed. Girls' hemlines went up and up, then suddenly they plunged, and the long 'maxi' skirt was all the rage. Within a few years boys' shoe styles changed from 'winkle-pickers' with long, pointed toes, to chisel-toes with the points chopped off, to elastic-sided Chelsea boots and then to Cuban (block) heels. By the end of the decade boys were wearing their hair long, and both boys and girls were in trousers with flared bottoms. The 'unisex' look had arrived.

In towns throughout the country small clothes shops, called 'boutiques', sprang up to sell the new styles. London, the 'swinging city', became the fashion centre of the world and, as Angela Turner remembered, the place to go was Carnaby Street:

The boutiques in Carnaby Street were amazing! The walls were painted in psychedelic colours, and there were false archways and pillars all over the place ... I bought a pair of white plastic knee-length boots.

The 'swinging sixties' swung to the beat of pop music: on records, on the radio, and on television in new programmes such as 'Top of the Pops'. In 1962 the Beatles emerged from the Cavern Club in Liverpool and, with their first album, *Please Please Me*, became world famous within a year. Other British groups followed, such as The Rolling Stones and The Who. By the mid-1960s pop music and fashion were two of Britain's most successful exports.

(top left) In the 1960s
newspapers began to issue
glossy colour magazines, full
of articles on design, fashion
and leisure. (left) Sizing-up a
mini dress outside a boutique.

A 'permissive society'?

Young people were not the only ones who wanted changes in the 1960s. There were some laws which, said many people, were out of tune with the times. In 1966 the death penalty for murder was abolished and in 1967, after a heated debate, Parliament changed the law which had made all homosexual acts a crime. Adult homosexuals could now behave as they wished in private. One Act made abortion legal in some circumstances, and another made divorce less difficult.

Opponents of these changes thought they promoted a 'permissive society', in which moral values were ignored and anyone could behave as they wished. Supporters argued that they made Britain a more tolerant place. In 1970 Parliament passed a law which reflected a change in the state's attitude to young people. The age at which someone legally became an adult was reduced from twenty-one to eighteen.

Students protesting outside the London School of Economics, in 1967. More young people than ever were going to college and university after school. When they disagreed with the rules, or the way they were taught, they would say so publicly.

A changing society

In the 1950s many people emigrated to Britain from newly independent Commonwealth countries (mainly India, Pakistan and the West Indies). Many were skilled people who did not realize that the jobs available for them in Britain were mostly low paid ones which they were over-qualified to do, for example in hospitals and on the buses. Although these were not jobs which the white population wanted, they accused black immigrants of taking their jobs, accepting lower wages and increasing the waiting lists for council houses. Sometimes highly qualified people were refused jobs simply because of the colour of their skin. In 1961 Sukhminder Bhurdi arrived in Britain from the Punjab in northern India, with a degree in science,

> I was turned down for all the posts I applied for. It was quite usual then for employers to say 'No thanks, we don't want blacks here'. In the end, I had to take work on the night shift in a car factory.

West Indian immigrants arriving at Victoria Station, London, in 1956. About 3000 arrived every month.

The Notting Hill Carnival was, and still is, held every August in London. It brought the Caribbean carnival tradition on to the streets of London, so black and white could celebrate together.

In the 1960s hostility to black people increased, and in 1967 a new racist political party, the National Front, was created. Racialist attacks became more frequent, especially against Pakistani families. Politicians in both main parties believed that the number of black immigrants from Commonwealth countries should be limited, arguing that if their numbers were not too great, white Britons would be more likely to accept them. Immigration Acts in 1962, 1968 and 1971 attempted to achieve this.

Meanwhile Parliament also tried to ensure that all citizens were treated equally. In 1965 a Race Relations Act made it illegal to turn people away from public places, such as pubs, on the grounds of their colour or race. It became unlawful to say or publish anything that might stir up racial hatred, and a Race Relations Board was set up to deal with complaints. In 1968 another Act made it illegal to refuse someone a job or to refuse to promote them because of their race or colour.

Northern Ireland

Since the creation of Northern Ireland in 1920 (see page 27), daily life for Catholics had become ever more difficult, as they watched Protestants being given priority in jobs and housing. The two communities held marches to commemorate important events in their history. Catholics, for example, paraded on the anniversary of the Easter Rising of 1916 (see page 22), while Protestants turned out on the anniversary of the 1690 Battle of the Boyne at which William III had put an end to the Catholic James II's hopes of regaining his crown.

In 1967 Catholics formed a civil rights movement to demand the same rights and freedoms as Protestant citizens, but a chain of violence started when Protestants attacked their marches. In 1969, with Northern Ireland apparently on the verge of civil war, James Callaghan, the Labour Home Secretary, ordered British troops on to the streets to restore order. At first the Catholics welcomed them.

The RUC was disarmed and the hated part-time Protestant force, the B-specials, was abolished. The government promised to speed up civil rights reform. Encouraged, many Catholics hoped that the recently founded Social Democratic and Labour Party would achieve further change by non-violent, political methods. However, the Irish Republican Army (IRA) was waiting on the sidelines. Since 1962 it had been concentrating on a political campaign for a united Ireland. Now it split in two groups. The Official IRA wanted to continue to work politically. The Provisional IRA wanted to return to an armed struggle and to protect Catholic areas from both Protestants and the police.

It was the British army's task to stop the Provisionals. As they searched for weapons and rounded up terrorists in Catholic homes (which they

often damaged), the troops were no longer seen as friendly protectors, but as hated aggressors. To Catholics it appeared obvious that the army was in Northern Ireland to maintain Protestant supremacy. As violence on the streets increased, the British government decided that, to prevent civil war, it had to rule Northern Ireland directly from London

All attempts to persuade Northern Ireland politicians to discuss alternative forms of government failed. As the IRA intensified its bombing campaigns, the citizens of Northern Ireland seemed doomed to suffer a cycle of violence which no one had the power to break.

'Bloody Sunday', 30 January 1972. Catholics in Londonderry held a civil rights march. British soldiers put up barriers to prevent the march leaving the Catholic Bogside area. When the unarmed marchers threw stones at them, the soldiers formed snatch squads to make arrests, and in the process fired on the crowd, killing thirteen Catholic civilians and wounding many others.

Europe says 'Yes'

Towards the end of the 1960s it was no longer possible for everyone to find a job, but neither trade unions nor managers tackled the need to train workers to do new or different jobs. The unions insisted on old methods of working, which might employ more workers than were really needed. High wages made British goods more expensive. Workers were laid off as fewer goods were sold. As prices rose, the unions demanded ever greater pay rises to keep up. They began to back up their demands with damaging strikes.

In 1970 the Conservatives won the general election and Edward Heath became the new Prime Minister. He believed that a better future for Britain lay in close cooperation with her European neighbours. With de Gaulle out of the way at last (he resigned as president of France in 1969), Heath made Britain's third application to join the EEC. This time it was successful and Britain joined in January 1973.

However, Britain's problems remained. In 1974 the miners went on strike for higher wages for the second time in two years. Starved of coal, the power stations could not provide enough electricity for factories and homes. Heath had to reduce the working week to three days to save fuel. Finally, he called a general election and lost. The new Labour government allowed the miners to negotiate a large pay rise for themselves. During the election Heath had asked, 'Who governs Britain?' It now seemed to many that the answer was 'the unions'.

In 1971 there was a change in Britain's coins and notes. Out went the old currency based on twelve pennies to the shilling and twenty shillings to the pound. In came a new decimal system with 100 New Pence to the pound.

Conversion tables, and careful labelling, helped shoppers to understand the new money.

CHAPTER 6

Britain in doubt

❖

In 1974 vast oil fields were found in the North Sea off the coast of Scotland. Over the next twenty years the sale of oil abroad earned Britain £220 billion. However, most of the profits went to private companies rather than the state, because the government sold off the state's share of the oil industry in the 1980s. Many Scots were angry because, although the oil fields were in Scottish waters, most of the profits went abroad.

In January 1979 Britain was paralysed when a strike by national lorry drivers was followed by many more, including water workers, ambulance drivers, dustmen and even (in Liverpool) grave diggers. As uncollected rubbish piled up in the streets, people were deeply shocked by what seeemd a never-ending trail of decay.

Prices had shot up and strikes had become frequent, and now one million people had no job. The country was deep in debt. Although the discovery of oil in the North Sea had started to provide income, the government seemed to have no answer to the crisis.

In March the Prime Minister, James Callaghan, who had replaced Harold Wilson as Labour leader in 1976, called a general election. The new Conservative leader, Margaret Thatcher, promised a firm line with the unions and 'a change of direction'. The voters were won over. On 4 May 1979 she became Britain's first woman Prime Minister.

A change of direction

Margaret Thatcher was to remain Prime Minister for eleven years, longer than any previous Prime Minister in the twentieth century. Unlike most Conservative leaders, her family background was fairly humble. She liked to remind people that she was the daughter of a grocer in Grantham in Lincolnshire, and to put across her ideas by using homely examples. She said that a country's finances were like those of a family. A sensible family would cut back on expenditure rather than increase its debts. Yet previous governments had gone on spending when it was obvious the country could not afford it.

In 1977 the public enthusiastically celebrated Elizabeth II's Silver Jubilee. In 1981 it was thrilled by the 'fairytale' wedding, shown here, of her eldest son, Prince Charles, to Lady Diana Spencer. In the 1990s however, as their marriage failed, the image of the royal family suffered. Although the queen remained highly respected, many people disapproved of the behaviour of the younger members of the royal family, and thought they should live less lavishly. Princess Diana herself became a popular figure. In 1997, her death in a car crash in Paris was met by a huge outpouring of public grief.

Her government cut spending on services such as roads and houses, leaving yet more people without jobs. 'There is no alternative', she said. Business failures and unemployment hit the north harder than the south. People in inner cities suffered most, and there were some violent riots in 1981. Five years later a report by the Church of England, *Faith in the City*, described some of the worst housing estates. They were badly designed with, for example, 'packs of dogs roaming around, filth in the stairwells, one or two shattered shops, and main shopping centres a twenty-minute expensive bus-ride away'.

Thatcher insisted that 'the National Health Service is safe with us'; but she thought that people relied too much on social security benefits, and her government made it harder to qualify for many benefits. She believed that competition was the answer to Britain's industrial problems. If companies were free to compete, the good ones would flourish. She thought that nationalized industries, without competition, failed to provide a good service, and her government sold off many of them.

Thatcher infuriated the trade unions when her government passed new laws which took away many of their rights. In 1984 a national miners' strike tested her determination to stand up to them, but the government was well-prepared. The power stations had stocked up enough coal to keep them going for some time. The miners themselves were divided. After almost a year, most returned to work.

After 1987, however, Thatcher's plans began to run into trouble. A new tax to pay for local government, called the 'community charge' by the government and the 'poll tax' by everyone else, was opposed even by many in her own party. The success she claimed to have achieved, in sorting out the country's finances and creating prosperity, was disappearing. Each year the Chancellor of the Exchequer put money in people's pockets by reducing income tax. As people could spend more, and borrow more easily, more goods were sold and soon prices were once again rising out of control.

By 1990 many Conservative MPs had come to the conclusion that under Thatcher's leadership they would not win a fourth general election. She resigned and they chose John Major as party leader. He also became Prime Minister. Almost immediately he announced the abolition of the hated poll tax.

The Conservatives had now been in government for eleven years, but this was partly because of the weakness of the opposition parties. Since the mid-1970s the Labour Party had been split between those on the 'far left' and the traditionalists. The left, for example, wanted more state ownership of industry, and wanted Britain to get rid of its nuclear arms. The traditionalists argued that these policies were too extreme to attract voters. Two election defeats in the 1980s seemed to prove them right. Labour was no longer trusted.

In 1981 four senior Labour figures, appalled by the success of the far left within the Party, broke away to set up the new Social Democratic Party (SDP). By 1988, however, the SDP had dissolved. Most of its members joined the Liberals to form a new Party, the Social and Liberal Democrats (SLDP) with Paddy Ashdown as its new leader.

In 1988 the Labour Party also elected a new leader. Neil Kinnock was determined to throw off the influence of the far left and adopt more moderate policies. In 1992, however, the Conservatives under Major narrowly won their fourth successive election victory. It was not until 1997 that Labour, now led by Tony Blair and calling itself New Labour, achieved a landslide victory at the polls and returned to government for the first time for eighteen years.

In 1982 the Argentinian army occupied a British colony in the South Atlantic, long claimed by Argentina, called the Falkland Islands. Thatcher's determination to recapture them led to a war with Argentina. The military risks were high. A defeat would have caused her downfall; the victory was her triumph. Cheering crowds and small boats welcomed the troops of the Task Force when they returned to Portsmouth.

Technology and the environment

In the last quarter of the twentieth century rapid change affected every aspect of people's lives. In the countryside modern methods of cultivation transformed vast areas. The enclosures of the eighteenth century had created the 'patchwork quilt' appearance of hedge, field and wood for which much of the country became so famous; but from the 1950s farmers and foresters began to pull up hedges, cut down woods and drain lakes to create larger fields and increase the amount of crops and trees they could grow and sell. In the 1970s, once Britain had joined the EEC, this process increased. Chemical fertilizers, insecticides and weedkillers destroyed many wild plants and flowers. The countryside, which once had a quite different appearance in different regions, began to look the same everywhere.

In the 1960s most people had been sure that scientists and inventors had the power to make their everyday lives more convenient and comfortable. In the 1970s they realized that the effects of technology could be bad as well as good. Many people joined campaigns to protect the environment against industrial pollution. By the 1990s hardly a high street in the country was without its recycling bank for glass bottles, cans and newspapers. As the number of cars and lorries increased, more people worried about the effects of traffic exhaust fumes on their health (see page 11).

(above) Much of the countryside now looks like this, with huge fields growing the most profitable crops.

In 1976 the airliner Concorde 002 made its first passenger-carrying flight from London to Bahrain. It flew faster than the speed of sound (i.e. over 1888 kilometres per hour). Concorde was a joint development between Britain and France, begun in the 1960s. After the Second World War British scientists and engineers led the way in many other technological developments, including nuclear power stations, hovercraft and computers.

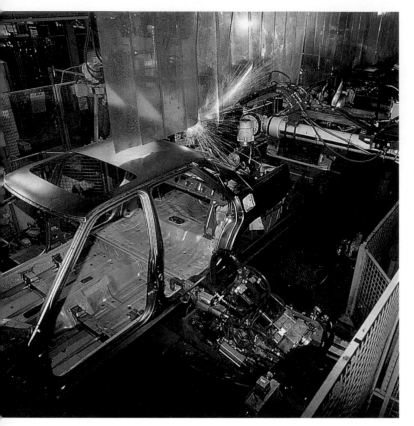

Robots, controlled by micro-processors, building Rover cars on an assembly line at Oxford. Unlike humans, machines can carry out assembly line tasks without tiring and without breaks. As automation increases, fewer people are needed for manufacturing tasks.

The microprocessor

In 1971 Ted Hoff, an American electronics engineer, made the technological discovery which was to have perhaps the greatest impact of its time on people's everyday lives. Hoff managed to place all the main electronic parts of a computer on a tiny slither or 'chip' of silicon. Twenty years earlier the tasks this chip, or microprocessor, could perform would have required a roomful of computer equipment.

The microprocessor opened the way to a new generation of gadgets including video recorders and pocket calculators. In 1980 hardly anyone had heard of a personal computer. By 1990 they were in common use in homes, schools and offices.

Microprocessors were quickly developed to be useful in every aspect of life. They controlled machinery ranging from washing machines to aeroplanes. They ran signalling systems on railways and guidance systems for missiles. As microprocessors took over many of the tasks usually done by humans, fewer people were needed in offices and factories. For people with skills and qualifications in fields such as computing and electronics, the future looked exciting. For people without them, it looked bleak. Already the new technology was creating its own divisions.

Theme park Britain?

During the 1970s and 1980s large parts of Britain's old industries finally disappeared. In the 1940s Aneurin Bevan had described Britain as an island, 'almost made of coal and surrounded by fish'. By the 1990s most of the coal mines were shut and the fishing ports, from Cornwall to Scotland, were almost empty of boats. Many steelworks, shipyards and docks in Wales, Scotland and the north east had gone out of business. Some of these old industrial sites lay derelict. Others were redeveloped as places to live, work or visit. Many became the focus of a new 'heritage' industry, tourism.

Critics complained that Britain was being turned into a gigantic theme park, a place where people came to admire the relics of a proud industrial past, but where nothing new was created. Instead, in the 1980s and 1990s the British increasingly made money from the services they could sell, such as banking and financial services based in the City of London. Many thought the key to revival lay in education, and in training a workforce with the skills to work in new industries.

After 1976 education became the subject of fierce argument. Some people doubted whether young people achieved enough at school, and if the ideals of the all-ability comprehensive schools, which had largely replaced selective schools from the mid-1960s onwards, were answering Britain's needs. The Conservatives introduced a national curriculum with different versions for England and Wales, Scotland and Northern Ireland. Yet in the 1990s, the results of British school-leavers seemed worse than those of school-leavers in countries such as Germany and Japan.

From the mid-1970s the number of people without jobs grew steadily, to over two million people in 1980 and over three million in 1986. By 1999 it had fallen back again to below two million. Young people suffered most from the shortage of jobs. In 1993 one third of the unemployed were under twenty-five. No job meant no money, and that was serious enough; but it brought other problems too. Many unemployed people felt depressed and useless. The old idea that a job was for life had disappeared. People began to work for contracts lasting only a few years, and more people chose to work for themselves and be self-employed, rather than work for an employer.

Whitby, in Yorkshire, was full of trawlers in the 1960s (below) and almost empty in 1981 (bottom). Competition from more modern ships from other countries, EEC rules limiting the amount of fish that could be caught, and a fall in the numbers of fish in the sea because of 'overfishing' all helped to destroy Britain's fishing industry. There were 29,000 trawlermen in England and Wales in 1938, 16,400 in 1960 and only 11,000 in 1994.

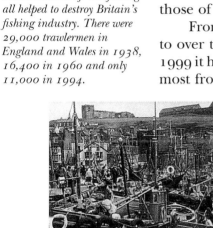

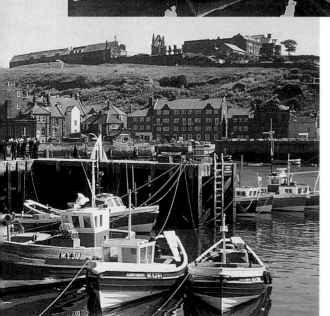

(right) Part of the Albert Dock in Liverpool. The dockyard was built in 1845 when Britain's sea trade was flourishing. It is surrounded by large warehouses, used to store the goods that passed through the port. As the sea trade declined in the twentieth century the dockyard became deserted, but in the 1980s it was developed as a tourist attraction, with the warehouses converted into shops, houses, offices and museums.

A divided society

Since the 1970s people have become more aware of the importance of a healthy diet and exercise. Healthfood shops have appeared. Sport and 'keep-fit' exercise have become popular. In the 1980s thousands of people trained to take part in marathon runs. This is the start of the 1989 Great North Run, at Newcastle upon Tyne.

Between 1970 and the 1990s, the British people as a whole became more prosperous; but there was a huge difference between the ways of life of those who had jobs and those who did not. By 1990 most families had a telephone, television and refrigerator. More than two thirds had a video recorder. In 1993 the British took twenty-three million holidays abroad, more than three times as many as in 1971. Trips to the countryside in cars became more popular and so did camping and caravanning.

Also more people went to the cinema, the theatre, concerts, museums and art galleries than twenty years earlier. The arts had become a British success story. Regional theatres such as the West Yorkshire Playhouse flourished, as did orchestras like the City of Birmingham Symphony Orchestra. Many British novelists were world famous. British actors and film-makers regularly appeared in Hollywood's Oscar nominations, and were internationally successful.

For some people, however, the arts were a luxury. At the end of the 1970s, surveys showed that more than ten million people lived either very close to, or below, the 'poverty line', the least amount of money the government calculated they needed in order to survive. Old people, one-parent families and people with disabilities were particularly likely to be poor.

After 1979 the gap increased between those who had much and those who did not. Ninety years after Seebohm Rowntree's first report his successors shocked the nation once again. 'The Rowntree Foundation today produces a picture of Britain that should make the blood run cold', reported the *Independent* newspaper. The report said that between 1979 and 1992 most people became wealthier, but the poorest tenth of the population became poorer. It pointed out that millions of people were losing hope of ever becoming prosperous again, and warned that many young people lacked the skills needed to do the new types of job available in a world dominated by the new technologies. If British society continued to be divided in this way everyone would suffer, for example, from crime and violence.

(below) Members of ethnic minority groups frequently complained that the police treated them unfairly. In the 1990s many police forces worked hard to recruit staff from ethnic minority groups.

(above) By the end of the twentieth century Britain had become a society of many cultures. These women are dancing at Navratri, a nine-day festival for the Hindu goddess Amba.

Different cultures

In the 1980s about one person in twenty belonged to an ethnic minority group. Most had been born in Britain and were the children or grandchildren of those who had been immigrants in the 1950s and 1960s. But they still faced many of the same problems met by their grandparents and parents. In 1976 the government gave powers to a new body, the Commission on Racial Equality, to look into complaints about racial discrimination. It was also made illegal for government departments and local councils not to provide equal opportunities for black and white people alike. Although this did improve things, black people were still more likely to be without a job than white people.

To be British in the 1990s could mean many things. A person might be, for example, Christian, Hindu, Jewish or Muslim, Scottish or Welsh, white or black. In many schools, where children came from a complete mixture of backgrounds, their different festivals and customs were celebrated. Children and young people, in particular, became much more aware of the different ways of life and beliefs in their society. Towns and cities reflected this diversity as Indian, Greek, Turkish, Italian and Chinese small businesses, shops and restaurants all became a natural part of Britain's high streets. Certainly there was tension and some violence, and Britain had not yet become a society in which all individuals mixed together as equals, but for many the schools pointed a way towards harmony and understanding.

A Women's Liberation march in London.

Equality for women?

Since the Second World War, the lives of many women had been changing. They had fewer children, thanks to contraception, so there was more money to go round. More women now had time for jobs; but the world of work was slow to respond. Not until 1970 did an Equal Pay Act say that within five years women should be paid the same as men for doing the same job. It was still assumed that women should marry and look after the children, while their husbands earned the money.

In 1975 the Sex Discrimination Act required that girls and boys should be given the same learning opportunities throughout their education, and that all jobs should be open to both men and women. An Equal Opportunities Commission made sure the new law was observed. Women began to work in careers which had previously been thought suitable only for men: as police officers, firefighters, jockeys, and airline pilots, for example, and many took up careers in business. In 1988 Angela Holdsworth, a television producer, wrote,

> Political parties, banks, industry now take women seriously and so do women themselves. They have become more assertive and confident.[Yet] one in eight families is looked after by women alone (as opposed to one in two hundred by men alone). There are few women at the top in industry or in any of the professions, and remarkably few in Parliament.

Nine years later, in 1997, a record number of 121 women were elected to Parliament, but even then only 18 per cent of all MPs were women.

Self-governing regions?

The loss of jobs in the old industries of Wales and Scotland made many people in these countries think they would do better on their own. Plaid Cymru, the Welsh nationalist party founded in 1925, won a seat in Parliament in 1966. The Labour government responded to Welsh discontent by giving the Welsh language equal status in law with English, and by arranging for the queen's eldest son, Charles, to be created Prince of Wales in a special ceremony at Caernarfon Castle in 1969. In Scotland nationalist feelings ran even stronger, and the Scottish Nationalist Party (SNP) won seats in Parliament as well as many local elections.

Most MPs from Wales and Scotland usually supported Labour, and the Labour government needed to keep that support. It decided to offer both Scotland and Wales some form of self-government. In 1978 Parliament offered to hand over certain powers from Westminster to elected assemblies in the two countries, provided the Scots and the Welsh agreed. The plans were dropped when both countries rejected them. In the 1990s the idea of special assemblies was revived and, in 1997, the newly elected Labour government put forward fresh proposals. This time a majority of voters in both Scotland and Wales accepted them. 1999 saw the first elections to the Scottish Parliament and the National Assembly for Wales. A question for the future was whether the different regions of England should also have more say in the running of their own affairs.

Northern Ireland

In Northern Ireland the story of bloodshed continued. There were also IRA bombing attacks on the mainland, including one against the Prime Minister herself and members of the Cabinet at the Grand Hotel in Brighton in 1984. Although the Protestant Unionists, whose MPs voted with the Conservatives in Parliament, might have expected Margaret Thatcher to be on their side, she saw that a solution to the position of Catholics could only come with the help of the government of the Irish Republic. Supported by all parties, and to the fury of the Unionists, she opened discussions with the Irish government.

The result, in 1985, was an Anglo-Irish agreement which stated that while Northern Ireland would remain part of the United Kingdom as long as a majority of its citizens wished it, ministers from Britain and the

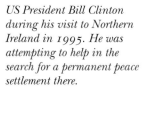
US President Bill Clinton during his visit to Northern Ireland in 1995. He was attempting to help in the search for a permanent peace settlement there.

Irish Republic would meet regularly to talk about matters of common interest. It was an historic moment. For the first time the British government recognized that the Irish government had some right to a voice in the affairs of Northern Ireland.

John Major continued to build on the relationship with the Republic. In 1993 he and the Irish Prime Minister, Albert Reynolds, published the Downing Street Declaration, which set out a joint approach to solving the problems of Northern Ireland. Behind the scenes secret contacts took place which led, in 1994, to the announcement of ceasefires, first by the IRA and then by the Unionist terrorist organizations. Despite occasional setbacks the ceasefires held, and the leaders of Northern Ireland's political parties began to negotiate a settlement that would once again give the province some degree of self-government. Eventually, in 1998, the Belfast Agreement led to the setting up, in 1999, of the Northern Ireland Assembly. Although there was still mistrust and many issues remained to be resolved, hopes for a permanent peace were higher than for many years.

In 1985 Bob Geldof, a pop singer, organized this 'Live Aid' concert at Wembley Stadium, London, and another in Philadelphia, USA. More than 1.5 billion people worldwide watched the concerts live on television. Together they raised £40 million to help feed people starving as a result of famine in Ethiopia.

Britain, Europe and the world

Abroad Margaret Thatcher shocked politicians in Europe by demanding a reduction in the amount Britain paid into the EEC. Like other members, Britain had her industrial wastelands, for example in the West Midlands and the north east, and money from the Community helped with new development. But overall Britain paid more into the EEC than she drew out. Suspicious that the increasing power of Europe might take away Britain's right to run her own affairs, Thatcher opposed proposals to create a common European currency and any suggestion that the EEC might one day become united politically. By 1990, despite her efforts, the UK government had lost a number of its powers to the EEC, which in 1993 became known as the European Union (EU). The press complained loudly when European laws over-ruled British laws in what often seemed to be unnecessary ways. In 1997, Tony Blair signalled that he wanted Britain to play a more central role in the EU. Like John Major before him, however, he chose not to commit Britain to joining the new common European currency, the Euro, at its launch in 1999. While the British were

A few moments after midnight on 1 July, 1997, British leaders ceremoniously hand over sovereignty of Hong Kong to China after 156 years of British rule. Hong Kong was one of Britain's last colonies. The ceremony was part of a long and significant change in world politics.

positive about some aspects of the EU, it was clear that they were cautious about how far they wished to be involved in others.

Beyond Europe, Thatcher and President Reagan of the USA shared many of the same ideas, including a loathing of communism. Indeed Thatcher's hostility to the communist East was so strong that the Soviets nicknamed her the 'Iron Lady'. Yet it was she who responded most warmly to the new Soviet leader, Mikhail Gorbachev, who wanted to end the Cold War and develop a new relationship with the West. 'I like Mr Gorbachev', she said, 'we can do business together'.

In 1990 the Cold War finally ended with the collapse of the Soviet Union. A new era of peaceful co-operation between East and West appeared to beckon, but it was soon clear that the ending of Russian authority in Central Asia would also create new problems there. The world seemed no more peaceful. British troops were involved in UN operations during the Gulf War (1991) and in UN and NATO operations in the former Yugoslavia throughout the 1990s. In 1997, Britain handed over to China one of her last remaining colonies, Hong Kong. It was a significant moment, for China was emerging as a new world superpower. What part would Britain play in this changing world in the next century?

CHAPTER 7

The twenty-first century

❖

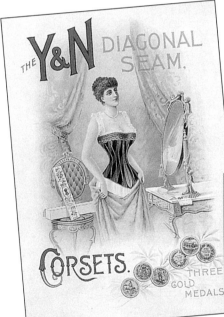

As the year 2000 approached, the British looked back over the twentieth century and forward to the twenty-first. In 1900 the writer H.G. Wells did something similar. He pointed out that more things had changed in the last hundred years than in the previous one thousand, and he asked himself what changes the next hundred years would bring. It is remarkable that at the start of the twentieth century someone should have been able to see so much of the shape of things to come.

In 1914 the government wanted to know how much it cost an ordinary working family to live. It worked out the price of a 'shopping basket' of typical everyday items. This included mutton, candles, back-lacing corsets and tram fares. Each year the government up-dated the items in the basket. In 1947 the new items included radios, bicycles, custard powder and cinema tickets. In 1956 in went brown bread, pet food, televisions and washing machines; candles and rabbits were dropped. In 1962 sherry and refrigerators were added. In the 1970s yoghurt and continental quilts were included, and in the 1980s, frozen oven-ready meals, video tapes and compact discs. In the 1990s out went tinned rice pudding, kippers, men's vests and the seven-inch single record; in went microwave ovens, camcorders and satellite dishes. The changes showed how, as they had more money to spend, people's lives were becoming increasingly comfortable.

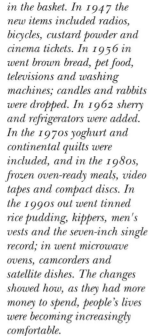

Changing lives

Wells predicted that the recently invented internal combustion engine would come to rival the steam engine. He imagined a new type of road surface suitable for cars and the development of motor trucks, motor buses and even motorways where, he said, 'streams of traffic will not cross at a level but by bridges.' Eventually, he said, motor transport would take over from the railways.

At a time when only a few people owned a telephone, Wells predicted that the land would be soon be criss-crossed by telephone wires and, in a hundred years' time, most people would use telephones to shop from home and to hold business meetings. The population would grow, and so would the towns, so much of the countryside would be built on. Houses would have central heating and buildings would be air-conditioned. Dirty coal-burning fires would become a thing of the past, and so would the armies of servants employed to clean the houses. All these changes happened just as Wells had thought they might, and there were many others too, beyond even his powers to foresee.

What kind of Britain?

In the late 1990s the British looked back at a century of rapid technological change; but it was also a century dominated by two world wars which left them twice victorious, and twice drained of money and resources. After 1945, although terrible things happened in other parts

of the world, Britain enjoyed an almost unbroken period of peace. The British experienced no famine, no volcanic eruptions, no earthquakes, no civil war. Only in Northern Ireland were there twenty-seven years of appalling violence and bloodshed.

Nevertheless, when the British read about how they compared with other industrial nations, they thought they were less successful. Britain had several problems to solve in the run-up to the twenty-first century. Perhaps the clearest was that the British were not rich enough to do everything they wished. If they wanted to play an important part in world affairs, they would have to spend money on armed forces. However, they also wanted the government to provide schools, hospitals and roads as well as a welfare state which was costing far more to run than its founders ever imagined. The answer was to either spend less or create more wealth.

Getting in touch has never been easier than at the start of the twenty-first century. Calls from mobile phones and text messages travel across the world via satellites in volumes that could never have been predicted.

An island nation?

During the twentieth century Britain's place in the world changed. She lost an empire and was replaced by the USA as the most powerful industrial nation. She became a member of the European Union (EU), but this brought problems as well as benefits. Membership of the EU meant that the British government had to give up some of its powers. While some people believed there were advantages to Britain in being part of a more united Europe, others disagreed and thought Britain should continue to run her own affairs politically, keeping only the trading links that were made in the 1970s. Many also feared that if Scotland and Wales were to become separate countries within the EU, the idea of a 'united kingdom' would disappear.

In 1994, meanwhile, the Channel Tunnel physically re-joined Britain to mainland Europe after a break of thousands of years. Britain was no longer an island. This was also true in another sense. Worldwide developments, in addition to the EU, were making it harder for the British government to control its own affairs. In the last quarter of the twentieth century, for example, many of the firms which made and sold goods in several countries grew much bigger. Some of these so-called 'multi-national' firms such as the USA's General Motors, Britain's ICI, or the media empire of the Australian, Rupert Murdoch, became so powerful they could even influence the decisions of governments.

Meanwhile, electronic mail and the worldwide web were shrinking the world still further. In the 1990s a person could sit in front of a screen at home and play video games with someone living in another town, and schools and scholars could talk to each other across the globe. Increasingly the British were living in a 'global village'.

Where the exchange of information once took days, the internet allows it to be almost instant. It has changed the pace of business and leisure and enables people from all parts of the globe to communicate freely. It has also triggered a move away from traditional employment as it allows workers to work from home, regardless of where they live in relation to their offices.

New century; new millennium

In the twenty-first century, as in every past century, the British will face old problems and fresh challenges. They have much on their side. In the twentieth century they not only gave all but a few of their colonies their independence, they also managed to stay on good terms with most of them. Britain is still well respected in the world and can offer much experience in world affairs. Meanwhile, at home, cities and towns have changed under the impact of immigration. The British are more aware than ever before of being a nation of many cultures and beliefs. There have been tensions and there are still problems to solve; but overall British society has been shown to be a tolerant one. Above all, since the 1970s, Britain has suffered the stresses and strains of high unemployment without seeing mass violence. Just as Britain was the first country to industrialize, so she has been the first to experience the collapse of the old industries and to start to come to terms with a new world, needing different skills and attitudes to work. It is a world full of opportunities.

As well as close of a century, the year 2000 marked the end of a millennium, the end of a thousand years. Two thousand years ago the British Isles were home to many different Celtic tribes. Within a hundred years all but those in Ireland and the very north of Britain fell under the power of Rome. A thousand years later, the Roman legions had long departed, and Saxons and Vikings from Europe were settled throughout the land. New kingdoms had emerged: one in England, a Scottish kingdom, several in Wales and many in Ireland. Over the last thousand years there has been one successful invasion by the Normans; national identities have been formed; kingdoms have been united and the Republic of Ireland created; the largest empire in the world has been built and then dismantled; great industries have been born; and a nation of country people has become a nation of town dwellers.

All over Britain and Ireland today we can see traces of life from those vanished times. They are to be found in earthworks and field patterns, in hedgerows and trackways, in stone crosses and churches. Who can tell what traces of our own lives will remain to be seen by our successors in a thousand years from now?

The earliest travellers to Britain told of white cliffs along the south coast. The cliffs still stand, but Britain is no longer an island.

THE ENGLISH ROYAL LINE OF SUCCESSION

❖

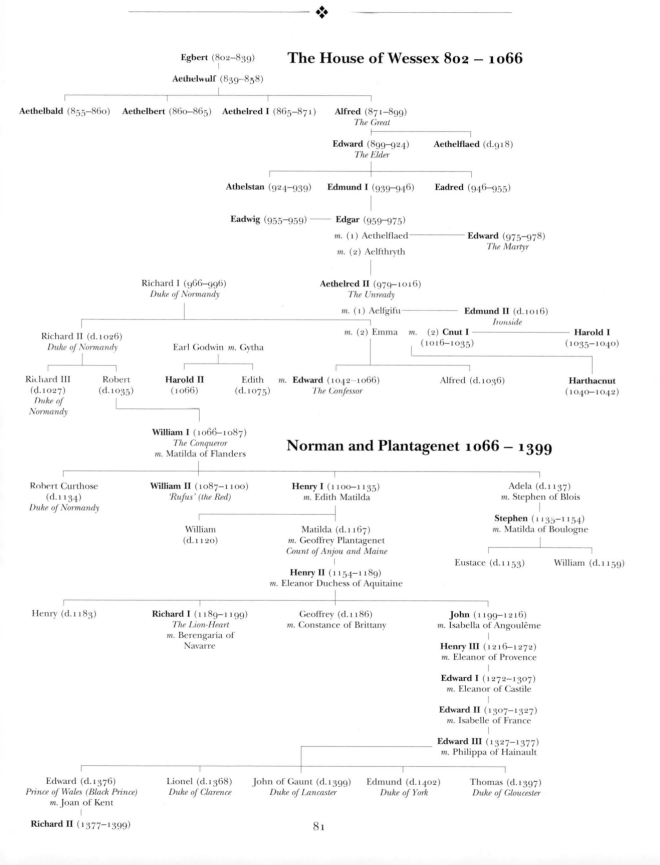

The House of Wessex 802 – 1066

Egbert (802–839)

Aethelwulf (839–858)

Aethelbald (855–860)   Aethelbert (860–865)   Aethelred I (865–871)   Alfred (871–899)
The Great

Edward (899–924)   Aethelflaed (d.918)
The Elder

Athelstan (924–939)   Edmund I (939–946)   Eadred (946–955)

Eadwig (955–959) ——— Edgar (959–975)

m. (1) Aethelflaed ——— Edward (975–978)
The Martyr

m. (2) Aelfthryth

Richard I (966–996)   Aethelred II (979–1016)
Duke of Normandy   *The Unready*

m. (1) Aelfgifu ——— Edmund II (d.1016)
Ironside

Richard II (d.1026)   *m.* (2) Emma   *m.* (2) Cnut I   Harold I
Duke of Normandy   Earl Godwin *m.* Gytha   (1016–1035)   (1035–1040)

Richard III   Robert   Harold II   Edith   *m.* Edward (1042–1066)   Alfred (d.1036)   Harthacnut
(d.1027)   (d.1035)   (1066)   (d.1075)   *The Confessor*   (1040–1042)
Duke of
Normandy

William I (1066–1087)

Norman and Plantagenet 1066 – 1399

William I (1066–1087)
The Conqueror
m. Matilda of Flanders

Robert Curthose   William II (1087–1100)   Henry I (1100–1135)   Adela (d.1137)
(d.1134)   *'Rufus' (the Red)*   *m.* Edith Matilda   *m.* Stephen of Blois
Duke of Normandy

William   Matilda (d.1167)   Stephen (1135–1154)
(d.1120)   *m.* Geoffrey Plantagenet   *m.* Matilda of Boulogne
Count of Anjou and Maine

Henry II (1154–1189)   Eustace (d.1153)   William (d.1159)
m. Eleanor Duchess of Aquitaine

Henry (d.1183)   Richard I (1189–1199)   Geoffrey (d.1186)   John (1199–1216)
The Lion-Heart   *m.* Constance of Brittany   *m.* Isabella of Angoulême
m. Berengaria of
Navarre   Henry III (1216–1272)
m. Eleanor of Provence

Edward I (1272–1307)
m. Eleanor of Castile

Edward II (1307–1327)
m. Isabelle of France

Edward III (1327–1377)
m. Philippa of Hainault

Edward (d.1376)   Lionel (d.1368)   John of Gaunt (d.1399)   Edmund (d.1402)   Thomas (d.1397)
Prince of Wales (Black Prince)   *Duke of Clarence*   *Duke of Lancaster*   *Duke of York*   *Duke of Gloucester*
m. Joan of Kent

Richard II (1377–1399)

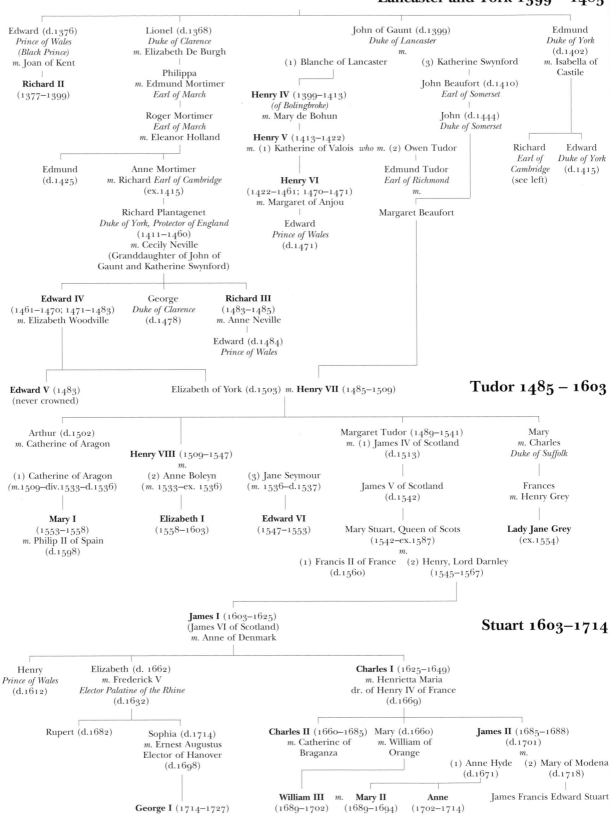

Lancaster and York 1399 – 1485

Edward (d.1376)
Prince of Wales
(Black Prince)
m. Joan of Kent

Richard II
(1377–1399)

Lionel (d.1368)
Duke of Clarence
m. Elizabeth De Burgh

Philippa
m. Edmund Mortimer
Earl of March

Roger Mortimer
Earl of March
m. Eleanor Holland

John of Gaunt (d.1399)
Duke of Lancaster
m.

(1) Blanche of Lancaster   (3) Katherine Swynford

Henry IV (1399–1413)   John Beaufort (d.1410)
(of Bolingbroke)   *Earl of Somerset*
m. Mary de Bohun

Henry V (1413–1422)   John (d.1444)
m. (1) Katherine of Valois *who m.* (2) Owen Tudor   *Duke of Somerset*

Edmund
(d.1425)

Anne Mortimer
m. Richard *Earl of Cambridge*
(ex.1415)

Richard Plantagenet
Duke of York, Protector of England
(1411–1460)
m. Cecily Neville
(Granddaughter of John of
Gaunt and Katherine Swynford)

Edmund
Duke of York
(d.1402)
m. Isabella of
Castile

Richard   Edward
Earl of   *Duke of York*
Cambridge   (d.1415)
(see left)

Henry VI
(1422–1461; 1470–1471)
m. Margaret of Anjou

Edmund Tudor
Earl of Richmond
m.

Edward   Margaret Beaufort
Prince of Wales
(d.1471)

Edward IV   George   **Richard III**
(1461–1470; 1471–1483) *Duke of Clarence* (1483–1485)
m. Elizabeth Woodville (d.1478)   *m.* Anne Neville

Edward (d.1484)
Prince of Wales

Edward V (1483)   Elizabeth of York (d.1503) *m.* **Henry VII** (1485–1509)
(never crowned)

Tudor 1485 – 1603

Arthur (d.1502)
m. Catherine of Aragon

Henry VIII (1509–1547)
m.

Margaret Tudor (1489–1541)
m. (1) James IV of Scotland
(d.1513)

Mary
m. Charles
Duke of Suffolk

(1) Catherine of Aragon   (2) Anne Boleyn   (3) Jane Seymour
(*m.*1509–div.1533–d.1536) (*m.* 1533–ex. 1536) (*m.* 1536–d.1537)

James V of Scotland
(d.1542)

Frances
m. Henry Grey

Mary I   **Elizabeth I**   **Edward VI**
(1553–1558)   (1558–1603)   (1547–1553)
m. Philip II of Spain
(d.1598)

Mary Stuart, Queen of Scots
(1542–ex.1587)
m.

Lady Jane Grey
(ex.1554)

(1) Francis II of France   (2) Henry, Lord Darnley
(d.1560)   (1545–1567)

Stuart 1603–1714

James I (1603–1625)
(James VI of Scotland)
m. Anne of Denmark

Henry
Prince of Wales
(d.1612)

Elizabeth (d. 1662)
m. Frederick V
Elector Palatine of the Rhine
(d.1632)

Charles I (1625–1649)
m. Henrietta Maria
dr. of Henry IV of France
(d.1669)

Rupert (d.1682)

Sophia (d.1714)
m. Ernest Augustus
Elector of Hanover
(d.1698)

Charles II (1660–1685) Mary (d.1660)   **James II** (1685–1688)
m. Catherine of   *m.* William of   (d.1701)
Braganza   Orange   *m.*

(1) Anne Hyde   (2) Mary of Modena
(d.1671)   (d.1718)

George I (1714–1727)

William III *m.* **Mary II**   **Anne**   James Francis Edward Stuart
(1689–1702)   (1689–1694)   (1702–1714)

Hanoverian 1714 – 1901

George I (1714–1727)
m. Sophia Dorothea of Brunswick-Zelle

George II (1727–1760)
m. Caroline of Brandenburg-Anspach

Frederick Prince of Wales (d.1751)
m. Augusta of Saxe-Gotha-Altenburg

George III (1760–1820)
m. Sophia Charlotte of Mecklenberg-Strelitz

Mary II (1689–1694)
m.
William III (1689–1702)
(son of Mary and William
of Orange)
(ruled alone from 1694)

Anne (1702–1714)
m.
George of Denmark
(d.1708)

James Francis Edward
Stuart
(*Old Pretender*)
(d.1766)

Charles Edward
(*Young Pretender*)
(d.1788)

George IV
(Regent from 1811
King 1820–1830)
m. Caroline of
Brunswick-Wölfenbuttel

Charlotte (d.1817)

Frederick
Duke of York
(d.1827)

William IV (1830–1837)
Duke of Clarence
m.
Adelaide of
Saxe-Meiningen

Edward
Duke of Kent
(d.1820)
m. Victoria of Saxe-Coburg

Ernest Augustus
King of Hanover
(d.1851)

Adolphus
Duke of Cambridge
(d.1850)

Saxe-Coburg & Windsor from 1901

Victoria (1837–1901)
m. Albert of Saxe-Coburg-Gotha
Created Prince Consort 1857 (d.1861)

Victoria (d.1901)
m. Frederick III
Emperor of Germany

Wilhelm II (d.1951)
The Kaiser

Edward VII (1901–1910)
m. Alexandra of Denmark

George V (1910–1936)
Duke of York
m. Mary of Teck

Edward VIII
Duke of Windsor (1936 Abdicated)
m. Wallis Simpson

George VI (1936–1952)
Duke of York
m. Lady Elizabeth Bowes-Lyon

Alice (d.1878)
m. Louis IV of Hesse

Victoria (d.1950)
m. Louis of Battenberg

Alice of Battenberg (d.1969)
m. Prince Andrew of Greece

Philip
(*later Duke of Edinburgh*)

Alix of Hesse
m. Nicholas II of Russia
(both ex. 1918)

Elizabeth II (1952–)
m. HRH Prince Philip
Duke of Edinburgh

Margaret
m. Antony Armstrong-Jones
1st Earl of Snowdon

Charles
Prince of Wales
m. Lady Diana Spencer
(d.1997)

Anne
Princess Royal
m.(1) Mark Phillips
m.(2) Timothy Laurence

Andrew
Duke of York
m. Sarah Ferguson

Edward
Earl of Wessex
m. Sophie Rhys-Jones

David
Viscount Linley
m. Serena Stanhope

Lady Sarah
Armstrong-Jones
m. Daniel Chatto

William   Henry

KINGS AND QUEENS OF SCOTLAND

❖

MAC ALPINE

843–58	Kenneth I
858–62	Donald I
862–77	Constantine I
877–78	Aedh
878–89	Eocha
889–900	Donald II
900–43	Constantine II
943–54	Malcolm I
954–62	Indulf
962–66	Duff
966–71	Colin
971–95	Kenneth II
995–97	Constantine III
997–1005	Kenneth III
1005–34	Malcolm II
1034–40	Duncan I
1040–57	Macbeth
1058	Luiach

CANMORE

1057–93	Malcolm III
1093	Donald Bane
1094	Duncan II
1094–97	Donald Bane
1097–1107	Edgar
1107–24	Alexander I
1124–53	David I
1153–65	Malcolm IV
1165–1214	William I
1214–49	Alexander II
1249–86	Alexander III
1286–90	Margaret
1290–92	No king

BALLIOL

1292–96	John Balliol
1296–1306	No king

BRUCE

1306–29	Robert I
1329–71	David II

STUART

1371–90	Robert II
1390–1406	Robert III
1406–19	Regent Albany
1419–24	Regent Murdoch
1424–37	James I
1437–60	James II
1460–88	James III
1488–1513	James IV
1513–42	James V
1542–67	Mary
1567–1625	James VI

In 1603 James VI became King of England, Wales and Ireland. From 1603 onwards the rulers of Scotland are the same as the rulers of England and Wales.

PRIME MINISTERS 1721–2001

1721	Sir Robert Walpole
1741	Earl of Wilmington
1743	Henry Pelham
1754	Duke of Newcastle
1756	Duke of Devonshire
1757	Duke of Newcastle
1762	Earl of Bute
1763	George Grenville
1765	Marquess of Rockingham
1766	Earl of Chatham
1768	Duke of Grafton
1770	Lord North
1782	Marquess of Rockingham
1782	Earl of Shelburne
1783	Duke of Portland
1783	William Pitt
1801	Henry Addington
1804	William Pitt
1806	William Wyndham Grenville
1807	Duke of Portland
1809	Spencer Perceval
1812	Earl of Liverpool
1827	George Canning
1827	Viscount Goderich
1828	Duke of Wellington
1830	Earl Grey

1834	Viscount Melbourne
1834	Duke of Wellington
1834	Sir Robert Peel
1835	Viscount Melbourne
1841	Sir Robert Peel
1846	Lord John Russell
1852	Earl of Derby
1852	Earl of Aberdeen
1855	Viscount Palmerston
1858	Earl of Derby
1859	Viscount Palmerston
1865	Earl Russell
1866	Earl of Derby
1868	Benjamin Disraeli
1868	William Ewart Gladstone
1874	Benjamin Disraeli
1880	William Ewart Gladstone
1885	Marquess of Salisbury
1886	William Ewart Gladstone
1886	Marquess of Salisbury
1892	William Ewart Gladstone
1894	Earl of Rosebery
1895	Marquess of Salisbury
1902	Arthur James Balfour
1905	Sir Henry Campbell-Bannerman

1908	Herbert Henry Asquith
1916	David Lloyd George
1922	Andrew Bonar Law
1923	Stanley Baldwin
1924	James Ramsay MacDonald
1924	Stanley Baldwin
1929	James Ramsay MacDonald
1935	Stanley Baldwin
1937	Neville Chamberlain
1940	Winston Churchill
1945	Clement Attlee
1951	Winston Churchill
1955	Sir Anthony Eden
1957	Harold Macmillan
1963	Sir Alec Douglas-Home
1964	Harold Wilson
1970	Edward Heath
1974	Harold Wilson
1976	James Callaghan
1979	Margaret Thatcher
1990	John Major
1997	Tony Blair

INDEX

❖

Bold page numbers refer to main entries; *italic* page numbers refer to picture captions.

A

Aberdeen 8, *31*
abortion 61
Acheson, Dean 56
advertising 7, 9, *10*, *12*, *33*
agriculture 14, *14*, 30, 67
aircraft *12*, 30, 67
World War II 40
alcohol 13
Aldermaston Marches 55
Anglo-Irish agreement 73–4
antibiotics *58*
art deco *30*
arts 70
Ashdown, Paddy 66
Asquith, Herbert 15, 17, 22–3
Attlee, Clement 45, *45*, 53, 54
Australia 36

B

Baldwin, Stanley 28, 29, 35
Barrie, J.M. 9
Barrow 8
Beatles *60*
Belfast 8
Belfast Agreement 74
Bevan, Aneurin 68
Beveridge, Sir William 45
Beveridge Report 45, 47
Bevin, Ernest 40, 53
Big Three 53, 55
Blackshirts *33*
Black and Tans 27
Blair, Tony 66, 74
Blériot, Louis *12*
Blitz 40, *40*
Bloody Sunday (Ireland) *63*
Bonar Law, Andrew 25
Boyne, Battle of the 62
Britain, Battle of 40
British Broadcasting Corporation (BBC) 34, 46, 57
British Expeditionary Force (BEF) 19–20
B-specials 62

Burma 42, 54
Butler, R.A. 45
Butlin, Billy 46

C

Callaghan, James 62, 64
Campaign for Nuclear Disarmament (CND) 55
Campbell-Bannerman, Sir Henry 16
Canada 36, *36*
cancer *58*
Cardiff 8
Cardus, Neville 47
Carson, Sir Edward 17, *17*, 19
Cecil, Lord *37*
Ceylon *see* Sri Lanka
Chamberlain, Neville 37–8, 39
Channel Tunnel 78
Charles, Prince of Wales 65, *72*
children's books 9
Christianity 57
Church of England 35, 57, 65
Churchill, Winston 13, 15, 37, 39–40, 42, 45, 51
cinema 34, *34*, 47, 57, 70
Civil Service 16, *41*
Clinton, Bill *73*
clothing 46, 60, *60*
World War II 'utility' *41*
coal industry 8, 28–9, 47, 63, 65
Cold War 75
Collins, Michael 27
colonialism 7–8, *7*, 35–6, *35*, *36*, 54
Commission on Racial Equality 71
common market *see* European Economic Community
Commonwealth, British 36, 42, 53, 54–5, 57, 61–2
communications technology 12, **48–9**, *48*, *49*, 51, 70, 77, 78, *78*
communism 53, 75
community charge (poll tax) 66
Compton, Denis 47
computer 49, *49*, 67, 68, *68*, 78
Concorde 67
conscientious objection *19*
Conservative Party 51, 56, 64, 66
Conservative and Unionist Party 17
contraception 72
Cook, Arthur 29
Coventry Cathedral 57

Crick, Francis 59
Curzon of Kedleston, Marchioness 8

D

Dáil Eireann 27–8
Davison, Emily 16
D-Day Landings 43, *43*
decimalization 63
de Gaulle, Charles 57, 63
deoxyribonucleic acid (DNA) 59
Depression (economic) 29–31, 35
de Valera, Eamon 28, 36
diet *31*, 51, *70*
frozen foods 51
World War I 23
World War II 41, *41*
Dig for Victory campaign 41
Dillon, John 23
Dimbleby, Richard *50*
diphtheria 58
Disraeli, Benjamin (Lord Beaconsfield) 15
divorce 61
dominions 36, *36*
Douglas-Home, Sir Alec 51
Downing Street Declaration 74
Dublin
Dáil Eireann 27–8
Easter Rising 22–3, *22*, 62
Dunkirk evacuation 40

E

Easter Rising 22–3, *22*, 62
economy 35, 57, 70
Depression 29–31, 35
post-war 46
Eden, Sir Anthony 51
education
Beveridge Report 45, 47
comprehensive schools 69
Education Act (1944) 45
free 25, *25*
grammar schools 45
national curriculum 69
secondary modern schools 45
technical schools 45
Edward VII 7
Edward VIII 35
Egypt 42, 55
Eisenhower, General Dwight D. 43

ACKNOWLEDGEMENTS

P6 Mary Evans; p7 Robert Opie; p8 Hulton; pp9t & b, 10tl Mary Evans; pp10c, 11bl Nat. Motor Museum; p10-11b British Motor Industry Heritage Trust; p11tl John Harrison/Still Pictures, cl Sainsbury's Archives; p12t, bl Mary Evans; p12-13b Mansell; p13tr London Transport; p14 Hulton; p15 Press Association; p16t & b Mary Evans; p17 Hulton; p18 ET; p19 Imperial War Museum; p20t Hulton; pp 20-1b, 21t IWM; p21tc Robert Opie, cr Falkirk Museums; p22 Mary Evans; p23 IWM; p24 Barnaby's Picture Library; p25 Bradford Industrial Museum; p26t Mary Evans, b Hulton; p27 Barnaby's; p28 Hulton; p29 Nat. Museum of Labour History; pp30, 32tl Arcaid; pp29t & b, 32cr Hulton; p32bl V & A; p33t Mary Evans, b Hulton; p34t Science & Society, b Ronald Grant Archive; p35 Robert Opie; p36 ET; p37 Hulton; p38 John Frost; p39cl, br Hulton; p40 AKG London; p41tl, bl Popperfoto, cr ET; pp43cr, bl, 44, 45br Hulton; p45tl IWM; p46 Popperfoto; p47t Ronald Grant, b Hulton; p48 tl Mary Evans; pp48b, 49c, br Science Photo Library; p48-9b BBC; p49tl Hulton Getty; p50t,b Popperfoto, c John Malam/Alphabet Studio; p51bl, c Robert Opie; pp51t, 52t Hulton; p52bl, br Retrograph Archive; p53 Hulton; p54 Camera Press; p55b Popperfoto, t & 56t John Frost; p56b Arcaid; p57 Bridgeman; p58tl Hulton, tr, br & 59tl, c Science Photo Library; p58-9b Popperfoto; p60-1tl The Sunday Times, tr Apple Corps Ltd, bl Barnaby's; p61t Press Association, b Hulton; p62 Barnaby's; p63t, b Popperfoto; pp64, 65 Rex Features; p66t Camera Press; p66-67b Adrian Meredith; p67tl Sally & Richard Greenhill; p68t Science Photo Library; pp68-69b, 69c, 70 Barnaby's; p69br Arcaid; p71tl Robert Harding, tr Greenhill; p72 Barnaby's; p73 Popperfoto; p74 David Redfern; p75 Popperfoto/Reuter; pp76, 77 (except tl & br) Robert Opie; p77 tl Science Photo Library; p77br Sony (UK) Ltd; p78 tl Hemera, bl Science Photo Library; p79 Telegraph Colour Library/Oliver Burston; p80 Life File.

All maps are by Hardlines, Charlbury, Oxfordshire.

Abbreviations:
BL = British Library; BM = British Museum; CCC = Corpus Christi College; EH = English Heritage; ET = E. T. Archive; IWM = Imperial War Museum; NG = National Gallery, London; NPG = National Portrait Gallery, London; V & A = Victoria & Albert Museum,